✳

the future

of advertising

New Media,
New Clients,
New Consumers
in the
Post-Television Age

joe cappo

AdvertisingAge
AdAge.com

McGraw·Hill

Chicago   New York   San Francisco   Lisbon   L
Milan   New Delhi   San Juan   Seoul   Sing

Library of Congress Cataloging-in-Publication Data

Cappo, Joe.
    The future of advertising : new media, new clients, new consumers in the post-television age / Joe Cappo.
        p.   cm.
    Includes bibliographical references.
    ISBN 0-07-146215-5
    1. Advertising.   2. Advertising—United States.   I. Title.

    HF5821.C34 2003
    659.1—dc21   2003041335

Dedicated to the memory of Gertrude R. Crain, 1911–1996.

2 3 4 5 6 7 8 9 0   LBM/LBM   0 9 8

ISBN 0-07-146215-5

Interior design by Steve Straus

McGraw-Hill books are available at special quantity discounts to use as premiums and sales promotions, or for use in corporate training programs. For more information, please write to the Director of Special Sales, Professional Publishing, McGraw-Hill, Two Penn Plaza, New York, NY 10121-2298. Or contact your local bookstore.

This book is printed on acid-free paper.

CONTENTS

PREFACE

At the time of this writing, I have been involved in some aspect of the advertising business for nearly thirty-five years. The first decade of those years I spent as a journalist, covering the business during what I believe included its most exciting and innovative years, starting in 1968.

A short time after I had joined Crain Communications as a columnist, the owners were reckless enough to appoint me publisher of *Crain's Chicago Business*. Although my colleagues in journalism might shudder at the idea, I actually was put in the position of selling advertising for the publication. We didn't call it selling, however; we called it "explaining the editorial product."

In reality, that's exactly what I was doing. Advertisers aren't buying the editorial product when they place an ad in a publication; they are buying the attention of its readers. Nobody should know those readers better than the editor of the publication. A good editor is a marketing expert at heart. He or she knows what the reader wants and can achieve this by many means, ranging from deep research to good, old-fashioned instinct.

After making dozens of calls with salespeople, I learned a few things that most journalists never realize. One is that sales is hard work, and I'm glad I've never had to make my living that way. I also learned there were salespeople who read my own publication and competing publications more closely than I ever did. They were getting intelligence to help them be more knowledgeable salespeople. It is a pity that there is often a disconnect between the editorial side and the business side of publishing.

Aside from covering and being involved in the sales process, I also have played the role of client, hiring and unhiring advertising agencies for *Crain's Chicago Business* and *Advertising Age*. That also lends a perspective from which advertising agency people might learn a lot. In reviewing agencies a few years back, the *Ad Age* management decided to look at different types of shops, from seasoned business-to-business agencies to hot creative agencies.

Here was the difference. The B-to-B shops, in my opinion, largely did their homework, examined our problems, and tried to propose realistic solutions we might use. But we encountered one creative hotshot—who shall remain unnamed—who thought he was going to be hired on the basis of his reputation. He came in all smiles and handshakes, played his reel of commercials, then gave us some lame campaign theme he apparently thought up on the cab ride over to our offices.

Obviously, he didn't get the assignment. He made the mistake of believing you sell the sizzle instead of the steak. Too bad the sizzle doesn't curb your appetite or provide you with any nourishment. Advertising is problem solving. It isn't movie making. Which brings us to this point.

The notion for this book started in 1992 after I wrote an op-ed piece for *Advertising Age* suggesting that advertising agencies were facing an identity crisis. I didn't write the headline for the article, but the editor who did apparently got the idea. The headline was "Agencies: Change or Die; Huge marketing revolution upsets old rules." Needless to say, it attracted a bit of attention in the business.

When I attended the annual meeting of the American Association of Advertising Agencies a few months later, I was pulled aside by John O'Toole, then president of the 4As and retired chairman of Foote, Cone & Belding. I fully expected John, whom I had known for many years, to give me hell. He didn't.

"I am so glad somebody has finally said what nobody wants to hear," he told me. "You have put the subject on the table, and we've got to talk about it." What had slipped my mind at the time was that O'Toole, who had spent most of his illustrious advertising career at Foote, Cone & Belding, was a renowned critic of advertising. In 1981 he produced a book titled *The Trouble with Advertising*, which took issue with many advertising practices.

Giving evidence that he truly understood the delicate and tenuous relationship between consumer and advertising, O'Toole was once quoted as saying, "When executing advertising, it's best to think of yourself as an uninvited guest in the living room of a prospect who has the magical power to make you disappear instantly."

Advertising needs more people like John O'Toole.

It has taken me a decade to get from that *Ad Age* piece to this book for several reasons. Perhaps the most important was that I was engaged in corporate duties that didn't allow me the concentrated amount of time to turn out a book. I am accustomed to writing an eight-hundred-word column. A book can easily be equivalent to one hundred columns, a writing output of two years.

There was another factor. The change in the advertising business was happening almost too rapidly to chronicle in a book. Even when the writing is finished, producing a book still takes months. An author of a work intended to be current is at the mercy of accelerating change. As a case in point, the Bcom3 acquisition by Publicis Groupe was announced after I started writing and was finalized before I finished the manuscript.

In this age of instant and continuous news, that kind of time lag is difficult for a journalist to deal with. When I turned over the manuscript to the publisher, I dreaded that some further momentous change might take place that would make this work irrelevant. I hope that hasn't happened, but that is up to you to decide.

I owe acknowledgments to many people who helped me in gathering background for and producing this book. At the forefront are those who allowed me to use their views in the "Another Voice . . ." commentaries you will find at the end of chapters. Most of these originally appeared as "Viewpoint" op-ed pieces in *Advertising Age* over the last couple of years.

In gleaning these essays, my intention was to show that I don't consider myself the sole and ultimate authority on what is happening in the advertising business. My goal was to present many opinions from different sources, illustrating that advertising is at a transitional stage in its evolution, and that this is of concern to many observers and participants in the business, whether they agree with my views or not.

Thanks are due to several people who gave me insight into areas in which I did not have intimate knowledge or came up with suggestions that caused me to add new ideas or alter my approach to the subject. Among them are Keith Reinhard, chairman of DDB International; Eric Strobel, managing partner of The Partnering Group; Don Schultz, professor of integrated marketing communications at Northwestern University's Medill School of Journalism; Brian Williams, president-CEO of Element 79; Wally O'Brien, director general of the International Advertising Association; and David Verklin, CEO of Carat North America.

I am indebted to Max Kalehoff of comScore Networks and Michael Zimbalist of the Online Publishers Association for providing me with a considerable array of relevant research on the Internet and new technologies. Others who sat for interviews include Howard Draft (Draft Worldwide), Ian Reider (Antenna Research, Mexico), Clemente Camara (Clemente Camara & Associates, Mexico), Bud Frankel (Frankel & Company), Norm Goldring (founder of CPM Inc.), Jack Myers (*Jack Myers Report*), Peter Krivkovich (Cramer Krasselt Advertising), Gene Secunda (New York University), Tom Harris (PR master, consultant, and author), Joe Pisani (University of Florida), and John Emmerling (Emmerling Communications).

In addition, I don't know of anyone who is more aware of the industry's challenges than Burtch Drake, president of the 4As, and his senior vice president John Wolfe.

A special word of thanks must go to Fred Danzig, who was editor of *Ad Age* when I was publisher and has since retired. Fred was always ready to pitch in during those days. And he did it again when I asked for his perspectives—and a use of his "Viewpoint" piece—on the advertising business.

I also owe thanks to several Crain employees who graciously contributed to my work. They include Mark Mandle, head of our Chicago information center, who ferreted out many of the statistics included in this work, and Craig Endicott and Kevin Brown, who manage *Advertising Age*'s data center. You don't know how much effort and attention go into the mountains of data our company produces every year. If I have forgotten others, I apologize. I did try to keep good notes.

Thanks also to David Klein, vice president and publishing and editorial director of the Ad Age Group, for encouraging me to do this book in the first place, and Rance Crain, our president and editor-in-chief, for his support, financial and otherwise. I also owe a bow to my longtime assistant, Mary Hryniszak, who remarkably is still sane after all of these years.

This book would not have happened without the enthusiasm and perseverance of literary agent Cynthia Manson, who devoted a tremendous amount of time and effort to this project.

Finally, I must emphasize that any opinions, observations, and evaluations contained in this book are those of the author or of the sources quoted. They are not intended to reflect the views of the editors of *Advertising Age* nor the management of Crain Communications, Inc., of which I have been an employee since 1978.

INTRODUCTION

Reminiscences from a Skybox Overlooking the Advertising Arena

For most of the last half of the twentieth century, advertising was exciting and it was fun. The business was riding a boom that started after the end of World War II but whose roots really went back to 1929. That was, of course, the year of the stock market crash. This was followed by the Great Depression, which segued immediately into World War II in 1941.

During the 1930s, the marriage rate and the birthrate both declined substantially. Unemployment never dipped below 14 percent during the whole decade of the 1930s. For four straight years—1932 to 1936—it never went under 20 percent.

The Depression didn't end until we entered World War II. By the end of the war, the United States, as well as many other countries, had suffered through fifteen or more years of deprivation. Consumers couldn't afford to buy cars during the Depression, and they couldn't buy cars during the war because cars weren't being manufactured. The auto manufacturers, as well as many other companies, had devoted their assembly lines to the production of war goods.

By the end of the war in 1945, there was an unprecedented pent-up demand for a return to a normal way of life. This meant a huge increase in marriages (up 42 percent between 1945 and 1946), followed months later by an increase in the number of births.

It was the beginning of what would become known as the Baby Boom, the era between 1946 and 1964. While births averaged a little more than 2 million per year in the 1930s, they zoomed to 3.6 million in 1948 and 4.3 million in 1957, still the record for births in a single year. Eventually, more than 75 million Americans were born during the Baby Boom, and this age cohort has remained a key target of marketers throughout their whole life span. The demand by Boomer families for all kinds of goods, from cars to television sets, has been staggering.

It was the development of television that set the tone and the priorities of the advertising business for decades to come. Just as television brought Milton Berle and Edward R. Murrow into our living rooms, it also introduced another newcomer that is still with us: the television commercial.

The technology and the creativity may have been a little uneven, maybe even terrible, during the early days, but by the 1960s and '70s, Americans were seeing brilliant, memorable advertising for Alka-Seltzer, Volkswagen, Pepsi-Cola, Benson & Hedges, 7UP, and many other brands. Viewers watched the commercials as closely as they did the programming.

Agency creative directors like Mary Wells, Jerry Della Femina, and Bill Bernbach became celebrities. But more than merely creative people, they were also entrepreneurs building businesses that were to make all of them wealthy.

These were heady days in the advertising business. With the exception of 1971, when cigarettes were banned from television and radio, advertising expenditures grew steadily. An expansive glow radiated over the industry for decades. It was *the* place to work for hordes of young people who would sacrifice anything to get a job in advertising.

Young men with Ivy League educations would take jobs in the mail room, hoping to get the attention of higher-ups so they might migrate into the media or the creative department. College-educated women would take jobs as receptionists, at pathetically low pay, hoping against hope to move up into the professional ranks or maybe only find a husband in the business. (This is not a sexist remark but a candid reflection of the times.)

Most of all, it was fun and exciting. I was able to witness all of this from a unique catbird seat. From 1968 to 1978, I wrote an advertising, marketing, and media column, mostly for the *Chicago Daily News* and briefly for the *Chicago Sun-Times*.

This was the era of the legendary three-martini lunch. It actually was mostly legend, but in a few cases, it was harsh reality. Whether it was Ratazzi's in New York or the Wrigley Building bar in Chicago, ad people had their favorite watering holes.

This was a time, remember, when entertainment expenses were one hundred percent deductible, and there was little or no limit on entertaining. There was something like an entertainment ladder that set the rules of the business. Advertisers were at the top of the ladder, being wined and dined by ad agency people. Ad agency people, in turn, were regularly entertained by the media representatives. What was gratifying about this for me was that all three levels of advertising felt it was beneficial to entertain the small corps of journalists who covered the industry. In other words, we got a lot of free lunches.

Among the media, television seemed to spend more on entertainment than anyone else. Much of this occurred during the upfront season, the time when networks try to sell next fall's programming to advertisers.

I recall one such event in the early 1970s, when ABC-TV rented the ballrooms in both the Ambassador East and West hotels in Chicago. The event started with a cocktail party, accompanied by a jazz trio, for about three hundred people in the Ambassador East. After a reasonable amount of drinking, a team of miniskirted models (acceptable then) came through the room, carrying signs saying "Follow Me." Everybody did.

We marched across State Street, while Chicago police halted all traffic, and into the Ambassador West. The Guildhall in that hotel was set up theater style. Under each chair was a bucket of ice, an open bottle of champagne, and a champagne glass. This was to keep the crowd occupied while network execs were previewing the new shows.

When the presentation ended, the audience was ushered into an adjoining room where more cocktails were being served, along with hors d'oeuvres, all of which was accompanied by music from a rock band whose identity I can't recall. An hour later, the doors of the Guildhall were swung open again, and a massive sit-down feast was provided. I do remember the dinner music. It was provided by the legendary Stan Kenton Orchestra.

This may not have been the typical media party (or it wouldn't have made such a lasting impression on me), but it wasn't all that unusual during those years. I also remember when CBS took over McCormick Place, erected a replica of the "M*A*S*H" set, and had all of the stars of the television series roaming around, rubbing elbows with advertisers and agency executives. That was pretty heady stuff for an advertiser, who later might have been invited to travel to the West Coast and spend some time on the set while "M*A*S*H" was being shot.

Television networks weren't the only major entertainers of that time. The national magazines also did their share, but none of them entertained as lavishly as the Time Inc. group. *Time* magazine, for example, acquired the premiere rights to the Steven Spielberg movie *Jaws* in 1975. The company rented out the Esquire Theatre in Chicago, catered a lavish meal in the lobby for several hundred advertising people, then treated them to a screening of the heavily publicized movie, days before any paying member of the public could view it.

A lot of advertising people, including lucky me, also didn't see *All the President's Men* in a movie theater the way regular people did. We enjoyed a preview of the film in the comfortable confines of the Playboy Mansion, with Hugh Hefner sitting first-row center, flanked by *Playboy* models. Each advertising salesperson for the magazine had a group of advertisers and agency media buyers as guests.

This kind of entertaining might not have ensured that the advertiser would buy a schedule of pages in the magazine, but it might have helped. More than that, it was something a media buyer could casually mention later on in a game of competitive name-dropping.

This entertaining was really aimed at the middle echelon of advertising people: media buyers, account executives, ad managers, and the like. Another grand event was reserved for the upper reaches of agency management. This was the annual meeting of the American Association of Advertising Agencies, traditionally held at the stately and sumptuous Greenbrier Resort in White Sulphur Springs, West Virginia.

Virtually no real business was conducted at these meetings, but they provided an opportunity for agency owners to meet and mingle with other agency owners. In the 1960s, eight hundred or so people would attend the event, which included everything from a black-tie gala with superstar entertainment to golf on the well-manicured Greenbrier course—perhaps even including a round with club pro Sam Snead.

Media executives were invited to be guests at these meetings, and their role was to host a series of parties and receptions at various locations on the massive Greenbrier property. What was unusual in those days was that most of the entertaining was done by newspaper and magazine companies. The television networks did very little entertaining, and they sent very few or no representatives, even though they were already garnering a majority of the advertising dollars spent by the agencies.

Imagine a young journalist being invited to attend his first 4As annual meeting and learning upon arrival that the Greenbrier did not accept credit cards. They would be happy, of course, to send a bill to his office.

This get-together of the advertising community is still held annually. It is rarely held at the Greenbrier anymore. The event is more informal, and the attendance is half of what it was thirty-three years ago, another victim of the consolidation in the advertising industry.

There is still a lot of entertaining going on in today's advertising world, but it is definitely less alcoholic than it was thirty years ago. An ad person is more likely to attend a three–diet Coke lunch than a three-martini lunch. The big venues for entertaining usually involve trips to the Super Bowl or the Olympics, and these are often hosted by the media with the broadcast rights, especially for clients who have bought sponsorships.

No one can deny that the advertising business has changed dramatically since that era, as I hope to show in the following pages. It is no longer the "ad game," which was a popular way of describing it back then. Advertising has turned into a serious business dealing in billions of dollars. Ad agencies, once freewheeling entrepreneurial shops, have been consolidated into global marketing services companies run by professional business administrators, rather than professional advertising people.

The agencies' clients, of course, also have consolidated, becoming huge manufacturing-marketing complexes. More than a dozen corporations spend over $1 billion each on advertising, and three of them spend more than $3 billion each. At the same time, the media also have been taking part in the consolidation craze, producing international combinations of print, broadcast, cable, satellite, and Internet entities.

Advertising has largely become a big business with big players. Maybe because of that, it isn't as much fun as it used to be—and maybe never will be again.

CHAPTER 1

AND THEN THERE WERE FOUR

A Once-Entrepreneurial Business Consolidates into a Handful of Big Holding Companies

Within only a few years, the advertising agency business in the United States has transformed from dozens of independent, entrepreneurial, creative, and highly competitive shops into an oligopoly of four large publicly held corporations. There continue to be many small advertising agencies, but there are very few medium-sized agencies.

What happened is that the holding companies grew by acquiring the larger agencies, not smaller agencies, as we shall demonstrate in the following pages. This created a huge gap between the four major holding companies and the rest of the pack.

The fourth of these major holding companies was formed in mid-2002, when Publicis Groupe, of France, acquired Bcom3, parent of what was best known as the Leo Burnett Company. Publicis, along with the other holding companies—Omnicom Group, Interpublic Group of Companies, and WPP Group—now account for an estimated 55 percent of all global advertising and marketing expenditures.

This is a far cry from 1960, for example, when there were no publicly held advertising agencies. The first major agency to go public was Foote, Cone & Belding, which did so in 1964. Only sixteen months earlier, agency chairman Fairfax Cone had been quoted as saying, "I wouldn't want to be part of any agency that owed its primary obligation to stockholders." As agencies grew, going public was inevitable.

Even years later, there was a good deal of skepticism—if not downright disappointment—about agencies going public. One that preceded even Foote, Cone & Belding was Papert, Koenig, Lois. "In retrospect," flamboyant advertising figure George Lois told *Advertis-*

ing Age in 1973, "public ownership was the catalyst for destroying our partnership. People became rich quick and choked up. They started to think, 'We now have obligations to stockholders.' I always said, 'No. My obligations are to myself and to my clients, to sell their merchandise.'"

Public ownership, although it may enrich a company's founders, is not a guarantee of success or survival in the corporate world. Generally speaking, agency stocks have not appreciated very much over the years. One reason for this is that most marketing services companies own very little in assets. They have employees and they have clients, both of which have proved to be eminently mobile in the advertising business.

Foote, Cone & Belding's sojourn as a publicly held entity is not the most positive part of its 130-year history. The agency was morphed into FCB Worldwide, which was a holding company, then transformed into True North Communications, and was eventually acquired by Interpublic in June 2001.

Foote, Cone & Belding was one of the oldest and most respected agency brands in the business, originally founded as the Lord & Thomas agency. Albert Lasker, known as the father of modern advertising, joined the agency in 1899 as a fledgling adman. Four years later, he bought into the agency and eventually worked on advertising for such accounts as Kimberly-Clark, Pepsodent, Sunkist, and Lucky Strike. Lasker got disenchanted with advertising in the late 1930s and retired in 1943, selling his share of the agency for $10 million (a fortune at that time) to Emerson Foote, Fairfax Cone, and Don Belding. Because of the pride of ownership, he would not allow the Lord & Thomas name to be used after his departure. And the Lasker name was never on the agency's door.

When I started covering the advertising business in 1968, Foote, Cone was the only sizable agency that was publicly held. All of the other leading agencies were still privately held enterprises. Some advertising people today may find it hard to believe that I, as a young journalist, actually knew the legendary Leo Burnett. I also knew Fairfax Cone, Bill Bernbach, Mary Wells Lawrence, Jay Chiat, Bill Marsteller, David Ogilvy, and many others who were running their own agencies. They were the "brand names" of the agency business.

I don't mean to imply that they were intimate friends of mine, or even that any of them could pick me out of a police lineup. But they existed. They were real people I might have met at the annual meeting of the American Association of Advertising Agencies (4As), during an interview for my column, or while attending receptions for their agencies or clients.

The advertising business was more personal then. The entrepreneurial head of an ad agency often had close personal ties, even friendships, with the entrepreneurial head of a major client.

Most of the contact today between major agency and major client is among midlevel managers on both sides. That is not the same kind of intimate relationship that existed decades ago. What changed this aspect of the agency business? Consolidation is probably the main factor. Agencies and clients have grown so large that those who run the companies are more involved with financial, accounting, and investment banking issues than with marketing issues.

THE BIG FOUR

By the 1970s, entrepreneurs who founded or took over agencies after World War II were ready to get out of the business and reap their rewards of ownership. A generation earlier, an entrepreneur would have turned over his business to a son or daughter. But the way to make big money in the 1970s and '80s was by going public or by arranging for an acquisition by another agency. That set the stage for the current lineup of four major holding companies.

To demonstrate how the agency business has been reconfigured during the past twenty years, I have taken *Advertising Age*'s list of the top twenty agencies—often called "agency brands"—in 1981 and updated the list to show their current ownership. All of them were independent agencies in 1981, although McCann-Erickson had already transformed itself into the Interpublic Group of Companies and was its largest business unit. Here are the 1981 standings, with the current ownership of each in parentheses:

1. Young & Rubicam (now part of WPP Group PLC)
2. J. Walter Thompson (WPP)
3. McCann-Erickson (Interpublic Group of Companies)
4. Ogilvy & Mather (WPP)
5. Ted Bates & Company (merged into Cordiant Communication Group)
6. BBDO International (Omnicom Group Inc.)
7. Leo Burnett Company (Publicis Groupe)
8. SSC&B (subsumed into Lowe & Partners, now Interpublic)
9. Foote, Cone & Belding (Interpublic)
10. D'Arcy MacManus & Masius (Publicis)
11. Doyle Dane Bernbach (Omnicom)
12. Grey Advertising (still independent)
13. Benton & Bowles (merged into D'Arcy, now part of Publicis)
14. Marschalk Campbell-Ewald (Interpublic)
15. Compton Advertising (subsumed into Saatchi & Saatchi, now part of Publicis)
16. Dancer Fitzgerald Sample (subsumed into Saatchi, now Publicis)
17. N. W. Ayer ABH International (subsumed into Bcom3, now Publicis)
18. Marsteller Inc. (merged into Young & Rubicam, now WPP)
19. Wells, Rich, Greene (out of business)
20. Needham Harper & Steers (Omnicom)

Of the top twenty agencies twenty years ago, seventeen have been swallowed up by the four major agency holding companies. One (Bates) is owned by the Cordiant Group, which may or may not become a major holding company, and one (Wells, Rich, Greene) went out of business after being involved in an unsuccessful merger. Thus, only one (Grey) is still an independent company.

At the time of this writing, there is ongoing speculation about the possibility of another major holding company being formed by a combination of two or more agencies under the Big Four. But any such courtship must always be done with an eye toward conflicts among competing clients.

In dollar terms, the four global holding companies had 2001 billings of $75 billion to $53 billion each. There is then a steep drop to the number five company, Dentsu, at $21 billion and Havas Advertising at $26 billion. But a little explanation of *Advertising Age*'s use of the term *billing* is in order.

Twenty years ago, billing represented the amount of media purchased by the agency for the client. It was a fairly easy number for journalists to ascertain and for readers to comprehend. Little attention was devoted to other marketing services. Since then, a couple of factors have changed. The first is that the actual buying of media is now assigned to media-buying agencies that may or may not be owned by the holding companies. The second change is the growth in marketing expenditures outside of the traditional media, such as sales promotion, direct marketing, and trade promotions. In today's environment, billing refers to the total marketing budgets of the clients or products assigned to the advertising agencies. Virtually everyone agrees that this is not necessarily an accurate measurement, although it does give some comparative values among agencies. In Table 1.1, the twenty-five largest advertising organizations in the world are ranked by gross income, rather than by billings.

ROOM FOR MORE?

Speaking at the annual meeting of the 4As in 2002, John Dooner, then chairman-CEO of Interpublic, asserted that the four major holding companies control 82 percent of the advertising billing in the

TABLE 1.1   TOP 25 ADVERTISING ORGANIZATIONS

This table ranks advertising organizations by worldwide gross income, including advertising agencies, public relations companies, sales promotion, direct marketing, and other non-advertising. Figures are for calendar year 2001 in millions.

Rank	Ad Organization	Gross Income	% Change
1	WPP Group	$8,165.0	2.5
2	Interpublic Group of Cos.	7,981.4	−1.9
3	Omnicom Group	7,404.2	6.0
4	Publicis Groupe (includes Bcom3 Group)	4,769.9	2.0
5	Dentsu	2,795.5	−8.9
6	Havas	2,733.1	−2.1
7	Grey Global Group	1,863.6	1.7
8	Cordiant Communications Group*	1,174.5	−7.0
9	Hakuhodo	874.3	−13.0
10	Asatsu-DK	394.6	−8.7
11	TMP Worldwide	358.5	−13.8
12	Carlson Marketing Group	356.1	−8.7
13	Incenta Group	248.4	13.6
14	Digitas	235.5	−18.3
15	Tokyu Agency	203.9	−11.3
16	Daiko Advertising	203.0	−10.2
17	Aspen Marketing Group	189.2	−24.0
18	Maxxcom	177.1	−0.1
19	Cheil Communications	142.0	−5.6
20	Doner	114.2	4.0
21	Ha-Lo Industries	105.0	−33.3
22	Yomiko Advertising*	102.2	−7.7
23	SPAR Group	101.8	−8.3
24	Cossette Communication Group	95.2	12.1
25	DVC Worldwide	92.6	4.4

*Advertising Age estimate.

Source: Advertising Age, April 22, 2002, p. 30.

United States. Although that is a commanding share of the business, it doesn't mean that the small and medium-sized agencies are going the way of the mom-and-pop grocery store. Many of the largest clients in the business still assign various projects and products to smaller agencies as they look for new ideas and strategies. Some of these assignments go to creative boutiques, others to sales promotion or direct-marketing agencies not affiliated with the Big Four. And, of course, there are thousands of small to medium-sized clients in the United States that don't want to deal with a huge ad agency. The other factor yet to be determined is whether all of the operating companies acquired by the Big Four in recent years will remain in the fold. There are bound to be defections, management buyouts, and other splintering along the way.

As Table 1.1 demonstrates, the traditional advertising agencies and their parent companies have invested huge sums to acquire operations outside of media advertising. They were a little late in realizing the growing importance of marketing activities outside of traditional advertising. And they still must prove that they are able to integrate the various marketing disciplines in order to direct a cohesive and coordinated marketing program for their clients.

This doesn't mean there isn't a need for huge global advertising companies. Everybody in the marketing chain is consolidating. Maybe it takes a Publicis–Burnett–Benton & Bowles agency to handle a Philip Morris–Miller–General Foods–Kraft–Nabisco client. Especially if the agency has to sell the client's products through a Time Warner Cable–AOL–CNN–*Fortune–People–Sports Illustrated*–WB–*Money*–CompuServe–MapQuest–Netscape medium.

If a client has a product to market globally, it has little choice but to deal with an agency offering global capabilities. The agency should be able to adapt the client's strategy to each marketplace, taking care to consider local customs, language, and sensibilities.

With the increasing number of international trade agreements, the need for agencies with international, if not global, capabilities has increased. Among agency brands, twenty or more have offices in more than fifty countries, led by the venerable McCann-Erickson, with 103 offices. These offices may be majority owned, joint ventures, or minority owned, but they still give an agency a presence in a country. In effect, the big agencies are in every market where there is a substantial advertising business. In addition to representing global clients in these markets, they are competing with local independent advertising agencies for local clients.

Figure 1.1 is a quick look at the major subsidiaries owned by the four holding companies.

Smaller agencies have banded together into networks. They may be able to handle occasional products that go international, but this is not an answer for those clients with serious designs on a global marketplace.

Will consolidation continue in the advertising business? It is likely, but not to the degree we have seen in the past twenty years. There is room for some combination of agencies that might include Havas Advertising, Cordiant, Grey, Dentsu, and perhaps Hakuhodo. But merging isn't necessary for their survival. There are plenty of local, regional, and developing clients that don't need global coverage and don't particularly want to work with the Big Four.

At least to one participant, there was little question about the immediate future of the advertising business. "I don't see how anyone else can now join the top tier," remarked Maurice Levy, chairman-CEO of Publicis, shortly after the acquisition of Bcom3. "I think the game is over."

Aside from that bravado, there is another reality in the business. The larger the holding companies become, the more room they make for individual entrepreneurs to develop their own businesses and serve new and small clients. The probability of spin-offs or management buyouts will also rise as the holding companies grow even larger. This is because the holding companies are made up largely of acquired companies rather than internal start-ups. It is not unusual for an acquired entrepreneurial firm to chafe under corporate management and seek to regain its independence. There may be oligopolies in advertising, but nobody has a monopoly on creativity or innovative strategy.

CLIENT CONFLICTS STILL LOOM

One of the reasons the four major holding companies continue to operate in so many different entities and individual agencies is an attempt to overcome the knotty problem of client conflict. Ford doesn't want its agency to handle Chevrolet, and vice versa.

The first time this challenge was tackled was in the early 1960s, when the "boy wonder" CEO of McCann-Erickson, Marion Harper Jr., decided to establish a holding company called Interpublic Group of Companies. Over the next couple of years, he acquired more than three dozen other agencies, including Jack Tinker & Partners, Erwin Wasy Inc. and Pritchard Wood, Inc., as well as public relations and promotion companies (*Advertising Age*, March 18, 2002).

The idea never really took hold. In 1967, because of a series of business reversals, the Interpublic board fired Harper, who maintained a low profile in the business world until he passed away in 1989. In *Advertising Age*'s 1999 special issue titled "The Century of Advertising," Harper was named the industry's second most influential person (after Bill Bernbach). Because of his revolutionary views, he was not admired by many advertising conservatives, and it wasn't until 1998 that he was admitted into the American Advertising Federation's Hall of Fame.

Despite Harper's early efforts, all these years later, client conflict is still a problem for agencies. In some cases, two separate agencies within a holding company can handle accounts from competing companies (but usually not head-to-head competitors). In this age of client and agency consolidation, the opposite is more likely to happen. Here's one ironic case.

FIGURE 1.1   PROFILES OF THE BIG FOUR

The four major holding companies have amassed substantial influence in the advertising and marketing business, largely by the acquisition of entrepreneurial operations. Here are profiles of the holding companies with a sampling of the entities they own:

THE INTERPUBLIC GROUP OF COMPANIES

Advertising Agencies
Avrett Free Ginsberg
Austin Kelley
Bozell
Campbell Mithun
Campbell-Ewald
Carmichael Lynch
Dailey & Associates
Deutsch Inc.
Fitzgerald & Co.
Foote, Cone & Belding
Gotham
Hill, Holliday
Howard Merrell & Partners
Lowe & Partners Worldwide
The Martin Agency
McCann-Erickson
   Worldwide Advertising
MPGH
Mullen
Suissa Miller
Temerlin McClain

Media Specialists
Initiative Media Worldwide
Universal McCann

Public Relations
Golin/Harris International
Weber Shandwick
DeVries Public Relations
The MWW Group

Specialized Communications
Draft Worldwide
NFO WorldGroup
FutureBrand
The Hacker Group

OMNICOM GROUP

Advertising Agencies
BBDO Worldwide
DDB Worldwide
TBWA Worldwide
Arnell Group
Element 79 Partners
Goodby, Silverstein & Partners
GSD&M
Martin/Williams
Merkley Newman Harty Partners
Zimmerman Partners

Media Specialists
OMD Worldwide
PHD Network

Public Relations
Fleishman-Hillard
Porter Novelli

Specialized Communications
Rapp Collins Worldwide
Alcone Marketing Group
The Integer Group
Tracy Locke Partnership
Doremus & Co.
Bernard Hodes Group

Source: Derived from the corporate websites: interpublic.com, omnicomgroup.com, wpp.com, publicis.com.

WPP GROUP

Advertising Agencies
J. Walter Thompson
Ogilvy & Mather
Y&R Advertising
The Batey Group
Marsteller

Media Specialists
MindShare
Mediaedge:cia
Kantar Media Research

Public Relations
Burson-Marsteller
Hill & Knowlton
Ogilvy Public Relations

Specialized Communications
Sudler & Hennessey
Kang & Lee
A. Eicoff
Uniworld

Branding, Identity, etc.
Landor Associates
Wunderman
Enterprise IG
The Partners
Millward Brown

PUBLICIS GROUPE SA

Advertising Agencies
Publicis Worldwide
Leo Burnett
Saatchi & Saatchi
Fallon
Bartle Bogle Hegarty (49% owned)

Media Specialists
Starcom Media Vest
Zenith Optimedia

Public Relations
Manning Selvage & Lee
Publicis Consultants

Specialized Communications
Burrell Communications
Conill Advertising
Pangea
Publicis Sanchez & Levitan
Tapestry
Medicus Group
Nelson Communications
ARC
Frankel
The Triangle Group

Interactive
Chemistri
Publicis Networks
Semaphore Partners

In 2001, True North Communications Inc. was acquired by Interpublic, whose largest client is Coca-Cola Company, handled by McCann-Erickson. True North is parent company of Foote, Cone & Belding (FCB), whose advertising assignments at the time included $400 million in business from Gatorade, Quaker Foods, some Frito-Lay products, Aquafina bottled water, and Tropicana and Dole juices. There was only one hitch: many of these products were part of the deal when PepsiCo acquired Quaker Oats Company.

Even though FCB was not handling Pepsi-Cola specifically, no Pepsi brand was going to be handled by a subsidiary of a holding company that also handled Coke. Pepsi had to split. As a result, a new agency called Element 79 (the atomic number for gold) was formed as a part of Omnicom, whose BBDO agency handles the Pepsi-Cola brand. About seventy-five former FCB employees switched over to Element 79 and continued working on the products they had been handling before.

This is not the end of the story. Shortly after forming Element 79, Omnicom also shifted the Lands' End account to the new agency. The tactic didn't work. Lands' End was acquired by Sears, while another Omnicom agency, DDB, is the primary agency for JCPenney. It didn't take Sears very long to put the Lands' End business up for a review. Client conflict may give accounts, but it also takes them away.

Does the principle of client conflict make sense? I think it does when individual brands are pitted against each other, like Coke versus Pepsi and Hertz versus Avis. Is it a conflict, though, if Procter & Gamble's disposable-diaper product is handled by an agency that is part of the same holding company as an agency handling Colgate-Palmolive's toothpaste? I guess it's up to the clients to decide. But with so much business being handled by only four major holding companies, clients will be severely limiting the selection of agencies that can work for them.

What the holding companies must do is erect firewalls between their subsidiaries, then stress that separation between them. This might work for tangential client conflicts, but I doubt any serious head-to-head competitors will want to be handled by the same holding company. Perhaps the most important issue in this conflict will arise over the unbundled media-buying entities that the holding companies have formed. Clients are just as concerned over security of their media plans as they are over their competitive strategy or creative work.

Who Killed the Giants?

JOHN EMMERLING

There is a large, ornate mirror in my bedroom that my wife got from the estate of Mary Lasker, widow of the legendary ad man Albert Lasker. I often look at its big, imposing surface and think about Albert—one of the first warlords of advertising—straightening his tie in the morning before striding out to some new conquest. In 1912, at the tender age of thirty-two, Lasker became the sole owner of the Lord & Thomas advertising agency. An opinionated tyrant who ruled with an iron fist, Lasker relentlessly drove his shop to become the largest agency in the world. (As a matter of policy, to keep things hopping, he would fire a certain number of employees every four years!)

The other morning, I worked up my courage and spoke to my mirror: "You in there, Albert?"

I heard the clearing of a long-dusty throat, then a booming voice: "Never thought you'd ask, son. Now, who are you—and what business are you in?" So I told him.

"Advertising, eh? How are my pals Ray and Bruce? And what's up with those new kids—Leo and Bill? And that English bloke, David?"

"Uh . . . I guess you mean Ray Rubicam, Bruce Barton, Leo Burnett, and Bill Bernbach . . . well, they should all be there with you," I said, not sure if my eyes should be glancing up or down. "And the English chap would be David Ogilvy—he retired to France years ago."

"Well, then," he growled, "who's kicking ass in the advertising business today?" I explained about mergers, acquisitions, and told him that accountants and financial people had become pretty important.

"Accountants are people who nudge numbers," he declared with annoyance. "I asked you who's kicking ass!"

"That's an interesting subject, Al," I stammered, stalling for time while trying to come up with a plausible reply. "Today, the term 'kicking ass' is sort of relative. The big ad agencies are headed by some very accomplished managers. They are smart, personable, and tend to have nice, straight, white teeth. You would find them quite polished—and they do make a lot of money on their stock options."

A disdainful grunt emerged from my mirror. "Tell me this, son—are these personable agency bigwigs able to take their clients by the hand and lead them into the marketplace jungle? Do they wrestle competitive advertisers to the ground and stomp 'em? Do they sit at the right hand of the client CEO?"

"Tough questions, Al," I mumbled. Then I rambled on about the growth of client marketing and research departments, about the incredible proliferation of media options, and about the development of global branding concepts.

"Son, I was asking you about the personalities of your leaders. Where are your tub-thumpers? Have you got any P. T. Barnums out there on Madison Avenue?" I explained that most agencies had abandoned Madison Avenue—and that very few tubs were still being thumped.

"How about the clients themselves—are any of them giants?" he asked with an almost wistful tone. "You must have some big, domineering clients who make headlines in the dailies and get splashed all over the cover of *Life* magazine?"

I was now backing away from the mirror. "Well, I guess there are a couple of client executives who could be called colorful."

"Like George Washington Hill of American Tobacco, right?" he continued, chuckling warmly as he recollected his old client. "George would spit on the conference table to make his point—so today's clients are still rambunctious rascals who need to be corralled, eh?"

"Not exactly, Al. No spitters these days. And very few clients are in ad agency corrals." I went on to say that his kind of "giants" tended to be found in related industries like media, entertainment, and technology. I told him about Ted Turner and Rupert Murdoch. ("My kind of guys," he grumbled approvingly.) I described the innovative deeds of Bill Gates and Steven Spielberg. ("Those smart, creative thinkers can actually be good business builders," he allowed.)

But he was relentless, returning again to his passion, ad agencies. "Give it to me straight, bozo—are you really saying there are no giants in the ad business today?" I frantically mind-searched my mental Rolodex . . . as I checked under *B* (for Biggies) I spotted a dozen prominent agency execs . . . but when I flipped to *G* (for Giants) the card file was bare.

"It seems, sir, we are definitely out of giants at the moment." Edging out the bedroom door, I promised to get back to him when the industry produced a genuine, high-profile ass-kicker. "I'll be here," he said, barely concealing his disgust.

Lately, I've started to avoid the mirror.

Actually, it's only a little inconvenient getting dressed in the kitchen.

John Emmerling, a longtime ad practitioner, is head of Emmerling Communications in New York (www.emmerling.com). This piece originally appeared as a "Viewpoint" article in the September 17, 1997, issue of Advertising Age.

CHAPTER 2

WHAT TO DO WHEN THE MONEY TREE DIES?

The 15 Percent Commission Is Gone, and Along with It the Primary Source of Agency Revenues

Being paid by collecting 15 percent of your client's expenditure on media is a lousy method of compensation. Yet that's how advertising agencies made their money during most of the twentieth century.

This practice started early in the history of advertising because agencies originally were agents of the media, not of the advertisers. Agencies bought space in bulk and at discounted prices from magazines and newspapers, then marked up the space and sold it to clients. In today's parlance, they would be known as advertising representatives, who still ply their trade for print media all over the world.

At that time, advertising was only a small part of the revenues generated by print media. Most of their income came from subscriptions and single-copy sales. Along the way, when print media saw that advertising could generate substantial revenues, they institutionalized the commission system, selling to recognized advertising agencies for 15 percent less than they would charge advertisers directly.

Although they were buying space in publications, clients had very little knowledge about what to say in their ads. This is where the agencies came into the picture. If they could create advertising that would move their clients' products, they would be able to sell more space and make more money. So they started producing copy and graphics for advertisements. After all, they were salespeople and knew how to sell, plus they were familiar with the audiences of the media.

Moreover, they didn't have to charge specifically for their creative services because they were making so much money reselling the space. As time went on, agencies eventually gave away public relations, sales promotion, research, strategic planning, and virtually every other service they could think of.

They could well afford to do this. They were still receiving commissions based on the amount spent on media. As media grew and proliferated throughout the twentieth century, agencies were still making their money from media buying. This became increasingly profitable with the growth of mass media, particularly radio in the 1930s and '40s and television in the 1950s and beyond. As audiences grew larger, rates increased, and agencies were pocketing 15 percent of much larger advertising budgets.

"Let's face it," said Keith Reinhard, chairman and CEO of DDB Worldwide Communications Group Inc., "We made a mistake a hundred years ago. We should never have been paid on the basis of how much media we bought. And when we asked the client if they needed a little help writing an ad, and we did it for nothing, it was a mistake."

Until the last decade of the last century, agencies were still living primarily off that commission, although clients were already negotiating lower commission rates. Agencies were also making a few bucks from the markup they added to the production work they bought for clients. This was modest enough when agencies operated in a print environment. But it became a substantial source of compensation (and often contention) in the broadcast era when the cost of producing a single television commercial could easily top $1 million.

HOW THE COMMISSION SYSTEM WORKED

Consider a typical situation in 1980 when an agency was assigned a shampoo account billing $50 million. A media director could make three calls to network television salespeople and ask for spending proposals to reach various slices of the audience. The agency creative director would hire a director to produce a series of television commercials with a budget of, say, $4 million. Within a few weeks, the agency could have walked away with a potential commission of $7.5 million from the media buy plus thousands more from the production markup.

As the cost of media increased in the 1990s—and a single spot on the Super Bowl would exceed $1 million or more—it became evident that clients were going to look for ways to cut costs. Agencies were already negotiating lower commissions on big media buys, but they weren't as low as the media-buying services that had already sprouted up in Europe. There had been media-buying specialists in the United States for many years, but most were small, and many specialized in buying specific media or combined media buying with media barter deals.

The U.S. media buyers often charged no commission at all. They existed on the spread between what they paid for media and what they could charge a client. The European media specialists, meanwhile, were buying time and space for 2 percent to 4 percent. In other words, a client with a 15 percent agency deal could trim as much as $13 million from a $100 million media buy.

That would leave plenty of money for the client to buy creative work, research, and other services on an à la carte basis from the agency. Full-service ad agencies responded by starting to negotiate commission rates with their clients. They also started exploring alternative forms of compensation, including hourly rates, retainers, and project fees.

REWARDING PERFORMANCE

It was only in the most recent years that agencies and clients started experimenting with incentive compensation based on the success of the advertising campaigns. This ultimately made good sense.

Agency compensation based on how much media the client bought was always a faulty idea. It is analogous to a sales manager paying the sales staff a commission based on how many lunches they bought for their clients. In the real world of business, salespeople are paid on how much they sell. At least a part of agencies' compensation should be based on the success of the campaign they created for the client.

Of course, advertising isn't necessarily in the real world. Clients hire agencies for many purposes besides selling products and services. They might also be trying to reposition a product, introduce a new product, resuscitate an old brand, develop a better public image, respond to a crisis, solidify market share, or meet any number of other objectives.

While it is not as easy and neat as paying a salesperson a certain commission on sales, it is still possible for clients and agencies to establish compensation criteria for results other than sales gains. A client and agency can identify the specific goals to be achieved by an advertising campaign. Through the use of various forms of research, they can determine whether those goals were reached.

What is interesting is that in the latter years of the twentieth century, many clients were just as reluctant as, or even more reluctant than, agencies to experiment with performance-based compensation. Why? Probably because they never had done it before and didn't see any reason to do it at that point.

But anyone who looks at this commission concept with the cold logic of business realizes that something else makes sense. For nearly a century, as clients were paying agencies a commission of 15 percent, those who got brilliant creative work paid the same fee as the clients who got uninspired work. And the agencies that produced effective advertising—the kind that boosted sales dramatically or introduced a new product successfully—got paid the same rate as those whose advertising bombed. Obviously, something was wrong with this business model.

ENTER THE MEDIA SPECIALIST

The traditional agency compensation system started eroding in the mid-1960s when a Frenchman named Gilbert Gross instituted the idea of bulk buying and started what is now known as Carat Worldwide, a part of the Aegis Group. Carat would make advance purchases of media at huge discounts from the rate card, then resell to clients. This, of course, is pretty much how advertising agencies started in the first place. Carat's concept of media buying caught on throughout Europe because it offered such economies of scale to clients.

The volume of business being done by media-buying specialists grew steadily in Europe, with the major interruption in that growth being the enactment of the Loi Sapin law in France in 1993. This law was aimed at eliminating hidden commissions and kickbacks that had become part of the media-buying business. By that time, however, a majority of the media buying in Western Europe was being accomplished through media specialists, eroding the earning power of traditional full-service ad agencies.

In 1980 media specialists were responsible for buying about 10 percent of the media in Europe. By 1994, their share had risen to 62 percent, with virtually all of the gain coming from full-service ad agencies. The percentage of media bought directly by clients remained at 6 percent during that span (*Inside Media*, April 26, 1995).

By 2001 Europe had reached a watershed. The World Federation of Advertisers conducted a survey of 450 advertisers in five countries—Germany, France, the United Kingdom, Finland, and Holland. Not one of the respondents reported paying advertising agencies the traditional 15 percent commission (WFA press release, September 24, 2001).

The question in the mid-1990s was whether the European media-buying concept could possibly get a foothold in the United States, which accounted for half of the world's advertising expenditures and where the client-agency relationships had been developed and nurtured for decades. The answer came quickly enough, although the U.S. version of media-buying specialists was different from Europe's. Rather than using independent and freestanding media-buying specialists, the traditional ad agencies unbundled their media-buying functions and spun them off into separate entities. N.W. Ayer & Sons, perhaps the oldest advertising agency in the world, made the first move in 1994, when it spun off its media department into a self-standing operation called Media Edge. This was eventually sold to Young & Rubicam. Within the next several years, WPP Group combined the media departments of J. Walter Thompson and Ogilvy & Mather and created MindShare; Omnicom developed OMD Media to handle buying for DDB, BBDO, and TBWA; Ammirati Puris Lintas Worldwide launched Initiative Media; and McCann-Erickson started Universal McCann.

By 2001 nine media-buying specialists were buying more than $10 billion each in worldwide media (see Table 2.1). Media buying by specialists in the United States amounted to almost $80 billion in 2001, up from $35 billion in 1998, despite the advertising recession of 2001 (*Advertising Age*, April 22, 2002). The most profound impact of the consolidation was felt by television, where nine major media buyers controlled more than 70 percent of all network television advertising sales (*Jack Myers Report*, March 18, 2002).

It would be wrong, however, to assume that the only function the media specialists were filling was that of negotiating better deals with television. As the number of media alternatives exploded, then began growing internally, it became evident that media buying had become a lot more complex than in earlier years.

TABLE 2.1 GLOBAL BILLINGS FOR THE TOP TEN MEDIA-BUYING SPECIALISTS IN 2001

Top Media Specialist Companies Ranked by World Billings	Headquarters	2001 Billings (in millions)
Initiative Media Worldwide (Interpublic)	New York	$20,987.0
MindShare Worldwide (WPP)	New York	20,300.0
Starcom MediaVest Group (Publicis)	Chicago	18,599.4
OMD Worldwide (Omnicom)	New York	18,224.1
Zenith Optimedia Group (Publicis)	London	18,076.0
Universal McCann (Interpublic)	New York	17,868.0
Mediaedge:CIA (WPP)	London	15,910.0
Carat (Aegis)	New York	14,677.0
MediaCom (Grey)	New York	11,600.0
Media Planning Group (Havas)	New York	8,750.0

Source: *Advertising Age*, April 22, 2002, p. S-14.

There was also the notion that larger media-buying entities could deal more effectively with the media companies that had already started consolidating. As media became unbundled from advertising agencies, the media people started to be far more creative with media. They developed strategies that did not automatically start with a major investment in television—a prejudice shared by many major ad agencies in the 1970s and '80s—accompanied by minor buys of other media to support the television campaign.

INTEGRATED MARKETING

Media-buying specialists rather quickly became more strategic and more creative in their thinking. For example, Carat Worldwide, the largest media company not affiliated with an advertising group, today creates campaigns that might include direct mail, Internet, outdoor, sales promotion, and other marketing functions that used to be considered "below the line" and were shunned by self-respecting advertising agencies.

As the number of media has proliferated in recent years, marketers have been able to focus on smaller segments of the market. This has demanded more research and insight from media buyers so they can reach the exact audiences needed to sell their clients' products.

David Verklin, CEO of Carat North America, maintains that there has been a not-so-subtle shift in how campaigns are constructed. Traditionally, an agency would develop a creative strategy, then assign its media department to buy the right media for that campaign. "Today, the media strategy often comes first, identifying the market," he says. "Then they develop the creative to appeal to that specific market." While advertising traditionalists may scoff, a younger generation of marketing specialists believes that this is a far more appropriate way to approach a marketing challenge.

It also corresponds with the increasingly popular notion of integrated marketing communications that every campaign should start with the potential consumer of a product, rather than with the manufacturer of that product. A marketer can reach a consumer only through the medium used by that consumer and only in a message that will prompt that consumer to respond. This is a lot different from blowing your advertising budget on a thirty-second spot on the Super Bowl, as several Internet-related companies—four of whom are no longer in existence—discovered in 2000 and 2001.

QUEST FOR REVENUES

It has taken only a few years for the major advertising agency networks to isolate media buying and remove it from its traditional spot as the money machine for traditional ad agencies. This has created a new challenge for the agencies: without media commissions, how do we generate income?

The answer to this has come in many forms. Agencies are now faced with the prospect of charging clients for services they formerly gave away. This is happening, although there is no one template for compensation that is as standard as the media commission was for most of the twentieth century.

The vast majority of agency-client contracts are based on a fee structure, while some still charge negotiated commissions based on media spending. Some agencies have developed hourly rate cards, similar to the way lawyers and accountants have operated for years. Others work on a project basis, sometimes with a performance incentive built into the formula. Some charge a retainer fee, plus service charges based on different criteria. A survey conducted for the Association of National Advertisers indicates that more than a third of the payment agreements include some kind of performance-based compensation element (*Advertising Age*, June 4, 2001).

There is, of course, still the markup on print and broadcast production. But none of these fees will ever generate the wealth that the 15 percent commission system produced in the good old days of advertising.

ANOTHER VOICE . . .

Clients Dictate Unkindest Cuts: Agencies Have "Rent-an-Employee" Mentality

PAUL S. GUMBINNER

About ten years ago, Marvin Sloves, then chairman of the agency Scali, McCabe, Sloves, told me about a layoff that his agency was contemplating. We were talking about who the layoffs might and might not affect when a specific name came up.

"Why, I wouldn't let him go if he were about the last person here. He has worked here for well over twenty years and deserves our loyalty," Marvin said. It was an incredibly humane statement and spoke well about the agency and its principles (and principals!). We aren't seeing too much of that these days.

The current round of layoffs has cut deeply without regard to past or, in some cases, current performance. In so many cases, employees have become a fungible asset, one employee having no more value than another. During this time of stress, economic uncertainty and diminished budgets, companies have taken on a "rent-an-employee" attitude.

The personal equity that is built by loyalty, past performance, and talent counts for very little. It seems that the bottom line has overwhelmed those other considerations.

Once upon a time, if a client cut a budget, the good people assigned to that business did not have to worry about their jobs. They knew that they would be rotated and moved to another opportunity elsewhere, probably replacing a poorly performing employee on another assignment. That doesn't happen much any more.

The downside of the fee system of agency compensation is that, to a great extent, clients are now running their advertising agencies. Often, fees are paid for a specific staffing plan. This, in effect, allows clients to dictate who will or will not work on their business. In fact, more and more clients even interview, or at the very least are consulted about, prospective agency hires for their accounts. And while agency management usually positions these interviews as a "courtesy," they are tantamount to giving the client tacit approval of prospective hiring.

This situation also works in the reverse when budgets are cut. When an account cuts its budget and staff cuts are made, it is often difficult to rotate people from one account to another. If a budget cut necessitates that a manager be eliminated, once upon a time this would enable an agency to evaluate all the employees at the level where the staff cuts were being made and, subsequently, to eliminate the weakest link on another piece of business.

Under today's fee system, when a client is happy with the performance of someone on its account it is more expeditious for agency management to leave an underperforming person in place than it is to explain to the client why it wants to remove a person with whom the client is comfortable. (Does any client really want to know that the person they perceive to be good is actually a poor performer?)

While there is no question that advertising budgets are down, necessitating staff cutting, profit pressures have exacerbated the situation. The publicly held companies, in order to meet shareholder expectations, are demanding a level of pretax performance that simply cannot be met. The result is a kind of "slash and burn" attitude on the part of agencies toward their employees, both good and bad, both high-performing and weak.

It is an easier management task to simply make staffing cuts by account than to re-evaluate the entire agency. Hence, a lot of good people are walking the street simply because their account cut its budget. I receive calls every day from really good people who simply expect to be fired because their account has cut its budget.

This should be a business where talent and ability far exceed temporary economic necessity or management expediency. All too many talented executives are walking the street for the wrong reasons.

Paul S. Gumbinner is president of Gumbinner Company, New York, an executive search firm serving the ad industry. This piece originally appeared as a "Forum" article in the December 3, 2001, issue of Advertising Age.

CHAPTER 3

ADVERTISING CHANGES ITS TUNE

The Industry Takes a Broader Look at the Form and Function of Marketing

There was a time, not that long ago, when advertising people considered themselves to be on a higher plane than any of the other marketing disciplines. They were arrogant because they commanded the lion's share of marketing dollars. They also were in a field that was more glamorous than such functions as sales promotion, direct marketing, or research. "Ad people used to think that sales promotion was tacky," one practitioner told me. "It wasn't as sexy as advertising."

Needless to say, advertising has changed its tune. This applies to the four major holding companies as well as to smaller agencies that realize advertising alone isn't enough to capture and keep clients. There is a difference, however, in how the various marketing functions are blended—or not blended—into an overall marketing campaign.

Wally O'Brien, former director general of the International Advertising Association, spent most of his career at J. Walter Thompson, starting in 1962 and eventually working his way up to vice chairman of the board. "At that time, J. Walter was quite an integrated agency. We had a merchandising department, a promotion department, and a public relations department that did work for many clients. We had thirty people in public relations," he explains.

These departments all reported to an account director, who dealt with the clients and coordinated the work on the assignment. The only unusual aspect about this, based on the current situation, is that clients did not pay for these services. The agency gave away these services because it was making enough from the 15 percent media commission to finance everything.

This is what we traditionally called a full-service agency. It was a one-stop shop where a client could get a product promoted and marketed. The only catch was that a substantial amount of money had to be put into media expenditure, especially television, to finance the campaign. For years, ad agencies promoted this concept of a full-service agency as they competed for marketing dollars with other marketing services providers, from creative boutiques to direct-marketing firms.

As the pressure mounted from clients to negotiate media commissions in the 1980s, the revenue derived from media buying started to erode. As a result, agencies started eliminating these services or started charging clients extra for them. This prompted clients to look at other options and to compare the agency's services in these areas with independent providers of specific services such as sales promotion and public relations.

There were plenty of independent companies that had huge operations in direct marketing, for example. They were not affiliated with full-service advertising agencies, and they had far more experience than most agencies could muster. They also didn't require that every campaign start by pouring a huge dollar amount into television.

Direct marketing has proved to be a powerful marketing tool, responsible for selling billions of dollars of products and services every year. It also has stood the test of time and technology. Years ago it was most commonly called direct mail. Direct marketers managed and manipulated huge mailing lists, through which they sent solicitations through the mail.

That is now only a part of the business. Those ubiquitous coupon ads in newspapers and magazines are part of direct-marketing programs. Telemarketing is another tool of this discipline, although it might also be the most disliked form of marketing by the American consumer.

While prime-time television was too expensive for most direct marketers, many found that late-night and early-morning commercial availabilities often went unsold. A shrewd direct marketer could make a deal to get a terrific price on a thirty- or sixty-second commercial. Better than that, some stations agreed to be paid on a per-inquiry basis, giving them a certain amount of money for each call that came into a special telephone number.

One of those pioneers in the field was the late Al Eicoff, founder and chairman of A. Eicoff & Company. In the mid-1970s, Eicoff told me that he had a specific reason for running direct-response commercials on late-night television. "People are less resistant at that hour," he contended. "They are more likely to respond to a call to action."

He also liked to run two-minute commercials rather than the typical thirty-second commercial because he felt the longer message was a more attractive lure. I don't know if his theories were correct, but Eicoff built a substantial business that continues to operate after his death. Now, however, it is part of the WPP Group, another indication of how the industry has consolidated.

Another form of direct marketing that has swept the world in recent years is the infomercial. Often for less than the cost of producing a thirty-second commercial, a production company can produce a thirty-minute infomercial and buy a block of time on a television station at a bargain rate. The products offered on these programs run the gamut from self-help tapes to quirky golf gadgets, compilations of old rock-and-roll songs, and virtually every kind of questionable exercise machine that is supposed to firm your butt or trim your abs. Celebrities are often paired with high-energy announcers to plug these products in settings that might include interviews with people who have used the products (or at least *claim* they have used the products) and staged demonstrations of the products, often repeated ad nauseam.

Although there has been considerable question about the success rate of infomercials, their appearance continues to increase. Much of this is because of the growth in cable channels, where late-night and Saturday-morning programs draw small audiences and would attract even smaller advertising revenues. This means the channel would rather sell the whole thirty minutes at a special rate to one advertiser than produce or buy a program and try to find sponsors.

On any given Saturday morning, as many as a dozen cable and satellite channels might be running infomercials at the same time. This is the case in most of the world. I have often seen U.S.-produced infomercials dubbed into other languages and broadcast anywhere from Europe to Asia to Latin America.

ADVERTISING'S NEW MEANING

The term *advertising* is used loosely these days, which is probably the best way to approach the business. It would be a misnomer to describe the four major holding companies simply as advertising agencies. With their current structures, they do far more than traditional advertising. Even their advertising subsidiaries are doing more than pure advertising.

At the 4As management conference in 2002, John Dooner, then chairman of Interpublic, stated that about 50 percent of the revenues of the four major holding companies come from activities outside of traditional advertising. Five years ago, he added, fully 90 percent of their revenues came from advertising. That is a tremendous shift in the way these companies earn their revenues.

There has been a long-term trend of promotional activities growing at a faster rate than traditional advertising. The actual numbers have been difficult to isolate, however, because promotion includes so many different functions. And unlike advertising, which is performed primarily by outside agencies, promotional spending is often done internally. In many cases, the budgets are not administered by the marketing department, but by the sales department of a client company.

Estimates of promotional spending are also difficult to ascertain because of differences in measurement methodology from one study to the next. So much promotion has been done internally that people in the promotion business believe the amount of promotion spending has always been underreported. Nevertheless, the outsourcing of marketing services to promotion companies has increased faster than advertising expenditures, and the major holding companies have acquired substantial operations in that field.

Table 3.1 shows the top sales promotion agencies in the United States. Note that the advertising recession of 2001 and 2002 did not spare them.

Until recently, the major agencies sniffed at most alternative forms of marketing outside of advertising. They contended that a client could build and nourish a brand only through advertising in the measured media. That argument obviously has been disproved many times in recent years.

Plenty of strong brands have been built with little or no advertising. Perhaps Starbucks is the ideal example. Not only has it established a solid brand name, it has a strong brand personality and a loyal following of consumers who will pay more for a cup of Starbucks coffee because they feel it is worth the extra money. The company has also been able to spread its brand name far outside the United States—to Europe, for example, and even to Asia, where coffee is not a traditional drink. More recently Starbucks has put its brand name on packaged goods sold in supermarkets. It has done all of this without a substantial advertising investment.

Starbucks can serve as the fantasy of any brand builder. But other retailers have been able to build brands without media advertising. Victoria's Secret has run its provocatively sexy commercials on television over the last couple of years, but it built its brand largely

TABLE 3.1	TOP TEN SALES PROMOTION AGENCIES, RANKED BY U.S. REVENUE FROM SALES PROMOTION

RANK   U.S. SALES PROMOTION REVENUE (IN MILLIONS)

2001	2000	Agency (Parent [Network])	Headquarters	2001	2000	Percent Change
1	1	Carlson Marketing Group	Minneapolis	$193.5	$228.1	−15.2
2	3	Euro RSCG Impact (Havas [Euro RSCG])	Chicago	142.1	168.4	−15.6
3	7	GMR Marketing (Omnicom)	New Berlin, Wis.	132.6	111.8	18.6
4	10	Momentum Worldwide (Interpublic [McCann])	New York	122.0	97.0	25.8
5	4	Jack Morton Worldwide (Interpublic)	New York	107.4	139.2	−22.8
6	8	SPAR Group	Tarrytown, N.Y.	97.7	104.7	−6.7
7	12	Integer Group (Omnicom)	Golden, Colo.	93.9	88.5	6.2
8	9	Frankel (Publicis Groupe [Publicis])	Chicago	89.8	99.6	−9.9
9	6	Alcone Marketing Group (Omnicom)	Irvine, Calif.	81.0	117.8	−31.3
10	11	Aspen Marketing Group	Los Angeles	79.4	92.6	−14.3

Note: Rank for 2000 is based on data reported to *Ad Age* in 2002.

Source: *Advertising Age*, April 22, 2002, p. S-14.

through its effective direct-mail catalog. The Body Shop, J. Crew, and L. L. Bean have also established strong brand identities without media advertising.

The Internet has also been successful in developing its own brands without advertising. Yahoo!, Napster, Google, eBay, and Monster.com are all good examples. Much of their success has come from the oldest form of advertising, word of mouth. The difference in today's media world is that the Internet spreads that word far and wide. Internet word of mouth should be a crucial factor to be studied and employed by brand builders of the future.

Is it possible for marketers of more traditional items like grocery products to build brands without advertising? Why not? Arizona lemonade was a hit before the company hired its first ad agency. So was Ben & Jerry's ice cream. Even President's Choice, a private-label identity—the antithesis of an advertised brand—has a strong brand presence in several product categories. All of these examples involve creating a buzz among the public and the media without any substantial advertising investment. That's what Botox acquired largely by word of mouth.

One common argument the advertising establishment made to clients in the 1980s and '90s went like this: You need advertising to build your brand. If you are using sales promotion techniques, you may increase sales of your product in the short run, but you are not increasing the equity of your brand. In fact, you may be damaging your brand's value by resorting to such tactics as couponing, price cutting, and sales inducements.

Now, after awakening fairly late to these marketing trends, the four behemoths of advertising are involved in virtually all of these nonmedia businesses. They have gotten there largely by acquiring literally dozens of public relations agencies, sales promotion companies, Web developers, direct-marketing firms, design and corporate identity companies, and the like.

Asked to describe themselves, the CEOs of the holding companies are more likely to say they are in the "marketing services" business or the "brand-building" business, rather than simply in the advertising business. Even more indicative of the new attitude of advertising toward the rest of marketing practices is the change in membership requirements for the American Association of Advertising Agencies. For decades, only full-service advertising agencies were allowed to join the organization. During those years, other forms of marketing were considered lowbrow, certainly not up to the status of media advertising. Worst of all were the media-buying specialists, considered to be the bottom feeders of the advertising business. Now all is forgiven. The 4As liberalized its membership rules in recent years to allow any element of the marketing industry to join, whether it be public relations, sales promotion, direct marketing, or, yes, even media buying.

Pragmatic as well as philosophical changes led to the liberalization of membership rules. Membership in the organization had been eroding for years because of the consolidation in the industry. This was exacerbated by the advertising recession that started in 2001, prompting agencies to cut back staff and scrutinize all kinds of expenditures.

LEARNING TO INTEGRATE

The major challenge for the Big Four is to learn how to integrate the myriad activities of these formerly independent companies into cohesive marketing strategies for their clients. Interviews with several participants and observers indicate that they are still a long way from offering truly integrated marketing services, combining media advertising with sales promotion or direct-marketing or telemarketing efforts.

Here's an example of how disconnected agency functions were when I was publisher of *Crain's Chicago Business* in the 1980s. At the time, we were lucky enough to have a particular client running both corporate advertising and direct-response advertising in the publication during the same time period. The account was handled by a major New York ad agency in conjunction with its owned and operated direct-response agency. The client had imposed a restriction in that it did not want a corporate and a direct-response ad to run in the same issue. But since the agency and the direct-response unit operated independently, it was *our publication's* responsibility to make sure there was no conflict, which we were careful to do.

One would imagine, though, that two affiliates of the same company should be able to coordinate its various efforts for a client. The two affiliates should have discussed timing of their campaigns in advance, especially since there is plenty of evidence that coordinated, bimodal forms of marketing often work more effectively than independent efforts.

Traditional advertising agencies have been beset by several challenges in recent years. One of them is the growth in influence of agency search consultants, a relatively new function. Clients considering the appointment of a new advertising agency often hire consultants to help them plow through the process. Most of these consultancies are run by former advertising practitioners.

One of the more mature companies in the field is Jones Lundin Beals, Chicago, run by Stan and David Beals (father and son), who call themselves "consultants in client-agency relations." The company conducted its first search in 1974, when such services were quite rare. The practice has become more formalized and more detailed in the intervening years.

The consultants usually start by assessing the client's needs, then prepare a request for proposals to a select group—or a cattle call group—of agencies. The typical search can be for a full-service agency, David Beals points out, but it can also be for a direct-marketing agency, public relations firm, media-buying specialist, or ethnic marketing specialist.

"This business has become more complicated now," Beals adds. "The notion of a full-service agency has changed. Our first step is to weed out any client conflicts among the agencies being considered. Even with the holding companies, many clients do not want to have any dealings with companies whose affiliated agencies are handling competitors."

Although every search is different, consultants often pare the list down to a handful of agencies and then let the clients make the final decision. Virtually all of the agencies are eventually paid on some kind of fee basis, and Beals estimates that 35 percent of the contracts have incentive clauses built in.

This may be the part that rankles agencies the most. "I don't mind filling out the forms and showing our qualifications to handle a piece of business, but I don't like them [consultants] getting involved in compensation," says one agency executive who asked to remain unnamed. "They are always trying to beat us down on fees."

The other complication in dealing with these consultants might be the cost to the agency, easily $100,000 or more, to produce presentations to show the consultants and clients that they can do the job. There are also the psychic wounds caused when the competition for an account becomes public and the agency that fails to get the business has to explain away that failure to its clients and other advertising people.

Perhaps nothing better demonstrates the revolutionary shift in the nature of agency-client relationships than a trend that has gained momentum in recent years. Many large advertisers, including Procter & Gamble, have appointed purchasing managers to work with their marketing departments to oversee and analyze advertising expenditures.

This movement indicates that clients are looking for some accountability from an area that historically has offered very little of it. Buying advertising services, of course, is not as quantifiable as buying janitorial services. The expensive price tag on a television commercial does not indicate in advance whether it will be successful.

There is no indication that the injection of purchasing executives has yet affected the advertising product, but the fact that clients are looking at this area far more closely than ever before simply puts added pressure on a business that is beset by pressures from all sides.

LOSING ITS GLAMOUR

As advertising has gone through all of these changes over the last twenty or so years, it also seems to have lost the image of being *the* place to be, an exciting business with plenty of freedom to be creative and innovative. Joseph Pisani, professor of advertising at the University of Florida and president of the American Advertising Academy, says there has been no drop-off in the number of students enrolled in advertising programs. "About 80 percent of our graduates go into some aspect of advertising, marketing, or sales after graduation. Probably 10 percent or less go directly to ad agencies. The emphasis in the past used to be on ad agency jobs, but that has changed because the jobs aren't there."

What is also lacking, Pisani says, is the great allure that advertising held for bright students decades ago. Many who might have formerly gone into advertising now start off in the sales end of the business. "I think it has hurt the agencies' creative product," he adds. "I don't see much creative breakthrough work, and that's what used to attract graduates."

Agency association president Burtch Drake confirms that agencies have been having difficulty hiring top college graduates. He suggests that advertising agency pay has generally been less than that offered by management consultants, client companies, and investment banking firms. Advertising, as everybody in the business realizes, was affected by a serious downturn in 2001 and 2002, but this is based on economic impact and is not the cause of declining interest in the advertising business.

ANOTHER VOICE . . .

New Media "Involvement Index" May Change Forty-Year-Old Marketing Rules

DOM ROSSI

At a time when America is running from advertising as fast as it can click, advertising return-on-investment depends on a new definition of "prime time." To be designated prime time, a medium must be capable of riveting its audience—and that connection must be measured.

There's an "involvement index" conversation now emerging within major agencies that's aimed at applying standardized audience-connection measurements to magazines. Similar data exist to do this for TV, radio, even the Internet. As ad people, we should jump at the chance to prove the connection of media on a level playing field. Only when we reverse the time warp of media will we reliably reach interested consumers when and where they're willing to engage, and thereby restore the intended value of advertising.

As it stands, marketing is out of step with the rhythm of modern life. The classical marketing rulebook was written forty years ago, when nuclear families convened at scheduled hours for meatloaf and Uncle Miltie. The advertising machine still follows the tenet of those times: if you wanted a lifetime brand relationship with America, and could afford it, you advertised to the enraptured masses in prime-time TV.

UPDATE STRATEGIES

Back then, a marketer's role was to get people to notice the brand. Today, it's to get them to spend enough time with the ad message to appreciate the brand's difference in a marketplace of unprecedented choice. This requires adapting communication strategies to the controlled chaos of modern life.

Peek in on the "average family" on a weeknight. One kid's got hockey practice, another a basketball game, a third her history-exam study chat on the Internet, and Mom's working late. Dad's posted a note in the kitchen—"Chicken, veggies, salad in fridge. Help yourself"—on his way out. Thankfully, the golden retriever has a doggie door.

When they do watch TV, "enraptured" hardly characterizes the routine tug of war over who controls the remote. They're too time-compressed, over-tasked and fractionated to function according to the TV network clock any more. Their lives have a rhythm all their own—a rhythm we marketers had better start to take seriously.

We can begin by recognizing prime time is no longer a "time of day." It's a frame of mind. Prime time is "my time," those prized moments when a consumer is tuned in to media and open to content. It may be a train ride, a nightly curl-up on the sofa, a truly engaging TV show, the half-hour in the parking lot waiting for kids' soccer practice to end. Whether or not it's on a schedule, the consumer is in control of it.

Astute marketers preach the imperative of "prime time" with consumers, yet our ingrained rulebook of marketing keeps us pouring the lion's share of budgets into national "prime-time" TV, despite audience declines (average 18–49 broadcast network ratings are down 45 percent since 1988) and zapping. Every so often, an advertiser creates a "whassup" that captures consumers' imagination. For most companies, though, that's tantamount to betting the future on one roll of the dice. They're paying prime rates but they aren't achieving prime time with consumers.

The irony in all of this is we send researchers around the world to understand every nuance about our consumers' lives except for how they interrelate with media. Consumer insights aren't often applied to the point of contact, where the big money is spent.

The solution isn't abandoning TV advertising. Nor is it expanding the list of public places where we chase our "targets," from movie theaters to bathroom stalls. It is evolving the purpose of the media machine—from getting attention to forging relationships.

A NEW MANTRA FOR MEDIA

For starters, "find the right frame of mind" should be the new mantra for media decision makers. Instead of attempting to wrest notice from consumers with meticulously produced film when they aren't really paying attention, we can consciously plan for connection. That connection starts with finding moments when consumers are willing to give us time to communicate a relevant message.

Research into consumers' lifestyles needs to include when and how they actually give dedicated time to advertising media. Frame of mind—when, where, and how consumers will engage—must set the parameters for the creative process. Media planning needs to synchronize the message with the medium. A fifteen-second spot can communicate a $1,000 rebate on a car that consumers already know, but a thirty-second ad probably won't communicate its driving characteristics versus the competition.

And, finally, media need to spend where the target-consumer involvement, not just audience size, is greatest. Only then can advertisers reasonably expect ROI.

While you may expect a magazine executive to question TV investments, don't miss the point: All media (and all communication plans) need to measure up to the involvement ideal. Media's the impact point of advertising, which remains business's primary customer-generating tool. It's up to all of us to reverse the time warp so we can catch up to consumers—on their turf, on their terms, and on their clock. Business is banking on it.

Dom Rossi (dom_rossi@rd.com) is executive publisher of U.S. magazines at Reader's Digest Association. This piece is from the April 29, 2002, issue of Advertising Age.

CHAPTER 4

DROWNING IN MEDIA

Proliferation Nibbles Away at the Power of
Traditional Mass Media

There is not a nation in the world—rich, poor, or in between— that does not have more media available to its citizens today than it had fifty years ago, ten years ago, or even two years ago. This worldwide proliferation of media is a major contributor to the revolution that is taking place in advertising and marketing.

Take my own rather mundane background as a media consumer. When I was a kid in Chicago at the end of World War II, our media world consisted of five daily metropolitan newspapers, a handful of AM radio stations, several national magazines, outdoor advertising, and movie newsreels. It seemed enough at the time.

Newsreels provided the medium by which most Americans actually saw the Japanese military surrender to Allied forces aboard the USS *Missouri* on September 2, 1945. Keep in mind that we didn't see this grainy, black-and-white film footage until days, maybe weeks, after the event occurred.

The only other source of news images came from photojournalism in newspapers and magazines, especially *Life* magazine. At that time, of course, there was no television. FM radio was for hobbyists and had few listeners. AM radio stations served the purpose that television serves today. Radio was our major broadcast medium, featuring the outputs of CBS, NBC, and the newly formed ABC network. There were also strong local radio stations in many markets.

THE BEGINNINGS OF RADIO

Radio was the mass medium that provided programming for everyone. There is virtually nothing on television today that was not bought, borrowed, or stolen from radio of the 1940s—news, sports, quiz shows, detective mysteries, cowboy adventures, soap operas, breakfast programming, situation comedies, dance music, variety shows, et cetera.

We listened to radio differently in those days, often in a family setting. Everybody could enjoy "Inner Sanctum," "Fibber McGee and Molly," "Lux Radio Theatre," and dozens of other programs that spanned the generations. It was not unusual for youngsters to sit with their siblings or friends and listen together to kid-oriented shows like "Jack Armstrong, the All-American Boy" or "The Lone Ranger." The broadcast day was filled with soap operas produced primarily for a female audience, the huge population of stay-at-home moms.

Nonetheless, radio was basically a mass medium aimed at everybody with ears. That's how television started its broadcast life, as a mass medium. Every program was intended to be watched by every viewer. This is the essence of a mass medium. The impact of television in the latter years of the 1940s and the early 1950s was unprecedented and overwhelming. It shattered the old media marketplace within only a couple of years.

Between 1949 and 1951, half of the movie theaters in the country went out of business. There was no reason to go to a movie house when you could watch movies in your living room for free. And the notion of going to a movie and watching a newsreel that was filmed two weeks earlier became ludicrous in the era of live television.

While the motion picture business was decimated, radio also was teetering on the edge of oblivion. It had lost much of its programming and most of its advertising to television. Americans were staying home at night to watch hit television programs like "Amos 'n' Andy," "The George Burns and Gracie Allen Show," "Our Miss Brooks," "Your Hit Parade," "The Life of Riley," and "Gunsmoke," all of which had migrated from radio.

Perhaps the most chilling shift for radio took place between 1950 and 1952, when Procter & Gamble moved virtually all of its massive advertising budget from radio to television, along with the soap operas its advertising supported. Radio was facing its darkest day.

The way we watched television in those early days was similar to the way we had listened to radio. The family was together in one room, except now the lights were turned out. Sometimes, extended families got together virtually every night to watch the flickering screen at the home of the first relative to spring for a pricey set. Others gathered at local taverns, which were early adopters of television as a way to attract customers. These were surely precursors of today's sports bars.

RADIO REINVENTS ITSELF

Fifty years later, however, radio is far healthier and wealthier than one would have guessed in 1952. Radio might well have gone out of business had it not been for one accomplishment: it reinvented itself. This is most evident in how listeners experience the medium today. Families no longer set aside certain hours to listen to radio. There is no big Philco console radio in the living room. Dad certainly doesn't want to listen to the alternative rock station that his daughter loves or the rap station that his son prefers. Similarly, the kids want no part of their father's favorite all-news radio station or their mother's all-talk format station.

Radio is no longer a social medium or a mass medium. It is a highly targeted individual and personal medium. The icon for this type of personal media consumption is the Sony Walkman and all of the other mini-portables of that genre. We listen to radio largely when we are alone. The earphones are on as we stride on the treadmill at the health club or travel to work on a commuter train. The radio is on when we are alone in our cars, listening for news or traffic reports while stalled in a highway traffic jam. A high school student will have the stereo cranked up while doing his homework . . . or not doing his homework.

Essentially, radio programming has evolved into little more than music and talk. To be successful, programming elements must be brief. People get in and out of their cars, on and off their trains, shift from treadmill to weight room. That's why hour or half-hour dramas or comedies don't work well on radio anymore. Even long symphonies don't work anymore—that is, if you are lucky enough to have a classical music station in your market.

Talk radio works because each question or comment lasts only a minute or two, then on to a different topic. I conducted a business commentary show on Chicago radio and other markets for eighteen years. It was a sixty-second commentary squeezed between a sponsor identification opening and a sixty-second commercial. Short and sweet. Make it brief; your listener is about to get off the StairMaster.

As opposed to seven or eight major stations fifty years ago, as many as fifty AM and FM stations attract substantial audiences in metropolitan Chicago today. Radio listeners have far more program choices today and are less likely to have one favorite station. New cars have fifteen or more preset stations, making it easier for listeners to switch from a news station to a soft-rock station to a sports talk station.

NEWSPAPERS: A MEDIUM IN TROUBLE

In contrast to radio, which is a totally different animal today than it was in 1950, another traditional medium, the newspaper, is essentially the same beast. The newspaper business continues to suffer because of competition from television and other new media. Newspapers have not reinvented themselves. Readers still get the same mix of local and national news, crime stories, sports scores, horoscopes, stock market listings, columnists for the lovelorn, recipes, and the rest. Adding color to a daily newspaper and increasing its coverage of weather are not deterrents to its ominous future.

The decline of newspaper readership is best exemplified by what has happened in Chicago. Only two metropolitan daily newspapers are left in the city, and both have fewer readers than they did fifty years ago, when there were four dailies in Chicago. Between 1950 and 2000, the *Chicago Tribune*'s daily circulation declined from 933,858 to 626,728, while the *Sun-Times*'s went from 629,000 to 468,170. This took place even though the metropolitan area's population has grown by more than 40 percent.

It is as if newspapers are operating in a vacuum and not recognizing that the rest of the world has gone somewhere else. Radio, television, cable, and now the Internet have all nibbled away at the newspaper's traditional role as the primary source of news and information. CNN, CNBC, Headline News, Fox News, ESPN, talk radio, all-sports radio, and America Online have all taken a bite out of newspapers. None of these existed fifty years ago or even twenty-five years ago. In a word, newspapers must change or die. They must redefine and reinvent themselves as radio has done.

Perhaps the main problem with newspapers is that they own printing presses. They act as if delivering information to their readers can only be done by putting ink on paper and trucking that paper all over a metropolitan area to put it in front of their readers' doors. Virtually all newspapers have websites, but most have failed to develop business models that will produce a decent yield from them. Not that this is an easy task. But as circulation continues to decline, newspapers should be undertaking some massive rethinking of their functions.

The Pew Center for the People and the Press remarked in a 2002 survey summary, "People are increasingly turning away from newspapers, but they have not given up on reading. Roughly a third said they spent time reading a book the previous day, no change since the mid-1990s. Americans under age 35 are more likely to read a book on a typical day than to read a newspaper."

TROUBLE FOR MAGAZINES

Magazines were also affected by the appearance of television on the scene. At first, smaller publications felt the impact of the tube. But by the early 1970s, the three huge stalwarts of American publishing, *Life*, *Look*, and the *Saturday Evening Post*, had all gone out of business. Like television, they were largely mass-circulation magazines aimed at the whole market.

With few exceptions, today's successful magazines are targeted publications aimed at particular demographic or psychographic segments of the market—niche audiences that want extensive coverage of their interests. This, of course, is exactly what advertisers are seeking for their niche products.

It could be said that the consumer magazine industry made a crucial strategic mistake during the early days of television. The mass magazines saw television as the enemy, so they erected defensive campaigns in order to keep advertising in their pages. What magazines should have done was to view television as another way to expand their brands. They could have become providers of programming for television. As a result of this attitude, there have been virtually no television programs based on magazine editorial content. Ironically, there are more magazines based on television than television programs based on magazines: *TV Guide*; *Soap Opera Digest*; *O, the Oprah Magazine*; and *ESPN the Magazine*, to name a few.

Like their brethren the newspapers, magazines are tied to the printing function, but they don't have the necessity of delivering to all of their readers every day. However, the proliferation of new magazines has also had an impact on circulation. Of the ten most widely circulated consumer publications in 1990, all of them had suffered declines, some substantial ones, by 2000. Single-copy sales for many magazines also plummeted significantly in that decade, another result of product proliferation without a corresponding increase in news-stand space.

Table 4.1 shows how the top ten magazines changed between 1990 and 2000.

CABLE VERSUS BROADCAST

For years, advertising was consumed with the five primary media: television, radio, newspapers, magazines, and out-of-home. Of these, television, hands down, was the favorite medium of advertising. Cable television started as a utility service, bringing network signals to out-of-the-way communities and other places that couldn't receive adequate over-the-air signals. But in the past twenty or so years, cable has started asserting itself as a source of programming in direct competition to broadcast television. Of course, from the viewpoint of the consumer, it's all television because the signal appears on the same television screen.

Cable operations have some structural advantages over traditional broadcasters because they have two sources of revenues, subscription fees from consumers as well as advertising income. The subscription fees totally support such advertising-free channels as HBO and Showtime, which in their own way are giving the traditional broadcasters fits, even though they carry no advertising.

The networks have always complimented themselves on producing great programming. But in recent years, HBO has garnered kudos from critics and the attention of millions of viewers through such original programs as "The Sopranos," "Sex and the City," "Six Feet Under," and a variety of televised specials. The return of "The Sopranos" to HBO in September 2002 marked a milestone for that network. The show attracted 13.4 million viewers, making it the most-watched HBO program in history. Even more significant, that

TABLE 4.1	CONSUMER MAGAZINE CIRCULATION	
1990 Rank	**Magazine**	**Circulation**
1	Modern Maturity	22,430,894
2	Reader's Digest	16,264,547
3	TV Guide	15,604,267
4	National Geographic	10,189,703
5	Better Homes & Gardens	8,007,222
6	Family Circle	5,431,779
7	Good Housekeeping	5,152,521
8	McCall's	5,020,727
9	Ladies' Home Journal	5,001,739
10	Woman's Day	4,802,842
2000 Rank	**Magazine**	**Circulation**
1	Modern Maturity	20,963,870
2	Reader's Digest	12,566,047
3	TV Guide	9,948,792
4	National Geographic	7,828,642
5	Better Homes & Gardens	7,617,985
6	Family Circle	5,002,042
7	Good Housekeeping	4,558,524
8	Woman's Day	4,244,383
9	Ladies' Home Journal	4,101,550
10	Time	4,056,150

Source: 1990 rankings: *Advertising Age*, June 24, 1991, p. S-2. 2000 rankings: *Advertising Age*, June 18, 2001, p. S-1.

episode of the crime drama attracted more viewers than any of the network television programs at that hour. That is a considerable accomplishment since HBO is in only about one-third of the television households in the country.

All of this has helped cable develop into a medium that is in more than 73 million U.S. households, or 70 percent of the country's total. In addition, at least 18 million households are equipped to receive television via satellite dishes. There is little question that cable and satellite are growing their audiences. The top dozen or so cable programs often draw larger audiences than the programming on the WB and UPN broadcast networks, according to Nielsen Media Research. But they also are creeping up on the more established networks.

There are several differences between cable and satellite, but the big difference for the advertising world is the number of individual channels available to subscribers. Most cable operators offer their subscribers about seventy-six channels. Satellite operations offer as many as three hundred channels. These include regular TV fare that's on cable, plus dozens of pay-per-view movie channels. (Unlike cable, satellite operators do not automatically carry all network and local over-the-air channels.) All of these additional channels have diluted the huge portion of the viewing market that had been dominated by network television.

Thirty years ago, the three major networks—ABC, NBC, and CBS—would regularly deliver 90 percent of the households watching television during prime time. But with all of the alternatives available to viewers, the networks—Fox included—might capture less than 40 percent of the households during any given week. Also helping erode some of the network audiences are the two minor broadcast networks, a sizable number of local television stations that thrive by offering movies or reruns of such popular series as "Seinfeld" and the "X-Files," and the Spanish-language networks, whose market is growing faster than the total television market.

Despite this dilution of their viewership, the networks are still charging advertisers top dollar for commercials because they are still producing the biggest mass audiences. There are advertisers who want to make major impact with their advertising. The best example of that is the annual Super Bowl telecast, which was attracting $1 million per thirty-second commercial in 1995 and more than $2 million for 2000. This per-commercial figure has settled lower in the last couple of years because of the general recession in the advertising market.

Not every advertiser, however, is trying to reach the huge, undifferentiated market. Some are trying to target their key audiences, something that cable and satellite can do more economically and regularly. A client that wants to reach a male audience to advertise its shaving product can buy time on a network sports program or on cable's ESPN. The networks generally offer sports programs only on weekends, while ESPN offers them twenty-four hours a day, seven days a week.

THE INTERNET COMETH

Just as television reshaped the media and advertising businesses in the 1950s, we now have the Internet starting to make a major impact on all forms of communications. This will be covered more thoroughly in Chapter 10, but it deserves a few words now because the Internet has added to the rapid proliferation of media in all markets of the world.

The Internet is building its own audience, siphoning users from all of the other media. In its most recent biennial study of trends in news consumption (released in June 2002), the Pew Research Center for the People and the Press reported that virtually all media had substantial declines in audiences since 1993, except for online news, cable TV news, and public radio.

In that period, respondents who considered themselves regular viewers of local TV news declined from 77 percent to 57 percent (see Table 4.2); of nightly network news, from 60 percent to 32 percent. Asked if they read a newspaper the preceding day, 58 percent said they did in 1993, compared with 41 percent in 2002. Those who considered themselves regular (at least three times a week) consumers of news on the Internet increased from zero in 1993 (when there was no World Wide Web) to 25 percent in 2002. By 2002, more people considered themselves consumers of cable TV news (33 percent) than of the nightly network news programs (32 percent). The study also reported that the dramatic growth in online news consumption has slowed down: "But the relative impact of online news remains substantial among those under 30, where online news has a larger following than any other format except local TV news" (Pew Research Center for the People and the Press, Survey R1, released June 9, 2002).

TABLE 4.2 TRENDS IN REGULAR NEWS CONSUMPTION

PERCENTAGE OF RESPONDENTS WHO REPORTED USING MEDIA

	May 1993	April 1996	April 1998	April 2000	April 2002
Local TV news	77%	65%	64%	56%	57%
Cable TV news	—	—	—	—	33
Nightly network news	60	42	38	30	32
Network TV magazines	52	36	37	31	24
Network morning news	—	—	23	20	22
Radio[a]	47[b]	44	49	43	41
Call-in radio shows	23[c]	13	13	14	17
National Public Radio	15	13	15	15	16
Newspaper[a]	58[b]	50	48	47	41
Online news[d]	—	2[e]	13	23	25

[a] Radio and newspaper figures based on use "yesterday."
[b] From February 1994.
[c] From April 1993.
[d] Online news at least three days per week.
[e] From June 1995.

Source: Pew Research Center for the People and the Press, June 2002.

What all of this means, of course, is that as more new media enter the marketplace, they tend to dilute the audiences for all of the old media. Far more media are available to me today than when I was a kid all those years ago in Chicago. We *all* have more media available. The only problem is that none of us has any more time to watch, read, or listen to it.

MEGA-MEDIA

One other aspect of the media world that must be addressed is the subject of consolidation. Just as four holding companies dominate the world of advertising and marketing services, a handful of media companies exert tremendous influence in several media categories. Walt Disney Company, for example, is best known for movie production but is also in television (ABC-TV), cable (ESPN), radio (ABC Radio Networks), and magazines (50 percent owner of *US Weekly*).

Table 4.3 describes the top fifty media companies, as tracked by *Advertising Age*.

There has also been some cross-border consolidation of media properties, but many countries have stringent rules regarding media ownership by foreign entities. This has served as a brake on growth in this aspect of the media business. Cross-border media ownership is more likely to occur in the area of print than in broadcast. And then there is the Internet, which is international by its very nature. It continues to develop rapidly in the major industrial countries, but also in every country in the world.

Finally, we must address the old saw that new media don't destroy old media. Radio didn't kill newspapers; television didn't kill radio, and so on. That is true . . . so far. But some new media are so disruptive that they force older media to change themselves radically in order to stay in business. Those that decide to circle the wagons and refuse to change, refuse to reinvent themselves, are almost certainly going to struggle to survive.

TABLE 4.3 FIFTY LEADING MEDIA COMPANIES, RANKED BY TOTAL NET U.S. MEDIA REVENUE IN 2001

| RANK | | Media Company | Headquarters | TOTAL NET U.S. MEDIA REVENUE | | | Worldwide Parent Revenue | Worldwide Net Income | NET U.S. REVENUE BY MEDIUM, 2001 | | | | | |
2001	2000			2001	2000	Percent Change			Newspaper	Magazine	TV	Radio	Cable	Other
1	1	AOL Time Warner	New York	$27,205	$24,957	9.0	$38,234	($4,921)	$0	$4,500	$445	$0	$13,542	$8,718
2	2	Viacom	New York	15,211	15,193	0.1	23,223	(224)	0	21	7,240	1,862	4,282	1,806
3	4	AT&T Broadband (AT&T Corp.)	Denver	10,329	8,855	16.6	52,550	7,715	0	0	0	0	9,799	530
4	3	Walt Disney Co.	New York/Burbank, Calif.	10,228	10,428	−1.9	25,256	879	0	212	5,166	547	4,303	0
5	7	Cox Enterprises	Atlanta	6,266	5,818	7.7	8,600	n/a	1,350	0	490	359	4,067	0
6	5	NBC-TV (General Electric Co.)	New York/Fairfield, Conn.	6,034	6,940	−13.1	125,913	13,684	0	0	5,360	0	674	0
7	8	News Corp.	Sydney	5,915	5,730	3.2	13,291	667	125	4	3,464	0	1,455	867
8	6	Clear Channel Communications	San Antonio, Tex.	5,703	6,093	−6.4	8,015	(1,144)	0	0	366	3,479	0	1,859
9	10	Gannett Co.	McLean, Va.	5,571	5,528	0.8	6,344	831	4,909	0	663	0	0	0
10	11	DirecTV (General Motors Corp.)	El Segundo, Calif.	5,550	4,694	18.2	177,260	601	0	0	0	0	0	5,550

(continued)

TABLE 4.3 FIFTY LEADING MEDIA COMPANIES, RANKED BY TOTAL NET U.S. MEDIA REVENUE IN 2001 *(continued)*

RANK		Media Company	Headquarters	TOTAL NET U.S. MEDIA REVENUE		Percent Change	Worldwide Parent Revenue	Worldwide Net Income	NET U.S. REVENUE BY MEDIUM, 2001						
2001	2000			2001	2000				Newspaper	Magazine	TV	Radio	Cable	Other
11	13	Comcast Corp.	Philadelphia	5,131	4,209	21.9	9,674	609	0	0	0	0	5,131	0
12	9	Tribune Co.	Chicago	5,104	5,577	-8.5	5,253	111	3,844	15	1,130	56	0	59
13	12	Advance Publications	Newark, N.J.	4,000	4,355	-8.2	4,000	n/a	2,025	1,975	0	0	0	0
14	14	Hearst Corp.	New York	3,986	4,136	-3.6	3,986	n/a	1,323	2,000	643	20	0	0
15	16	Charter Communications	St. Louis	3,953	3,249	21.7	3,953	(1,178)	0	0	0	0	3,953	0
16	20	EchoStar Communications Corp.	Littleton, Colo.	3,683	2,418	52.4	4,001	(215)	0	0	0	0	0	3,683
17	18	Cablevision Systems Corp.	Bethpage, N.Y.	3,064	2,998	2.2	4,405	1,008	0	0	0	0	3,064	0
18	19	Adelphia Communications Corp.	Coudersport, Pa.	3,060	2,557	19.7	3,525	n/a	0	0	0	0	3,060	0
19	15	New York Times Co.	New York	3,027	3,387	-10.6	3,016	445	2,826	0	128	13	0	60
20	17	Knight Ridder	San Jose, Calif.	2,900	3,212	-9.7	2,900	185	2,858	0	0	0	0	42
21	24	Bloomberg	New York	2,109	1,753	20.3	3,000	n/a	0	0	0	9	0	2,100

TOTAL NET U.S. MEDIA REVENUE　　　　　　**NET U.S. REVENUE BY MEDIUM, 2001**

RANK 2001	RANK 2000	Media Company	Headquarters	2001	2000	Percent Change	Worldwide Parent Revenue	Worldwide Net Income	Newspaper	Magazine	TV	Radio	Cable	Other
22	23	Washington Post Co.	Washington, D.C.	1,923	2,058	-6.6	2,417	230	843	380	314	0	386	0
23	22	Primedia	New York	1,922	2,129	-9.7	1,742	(1,112)	0	1,709	0	0	115	98
24	21	Dow Jones & Co.	New York	1,773	2,203	-19.5	1,773	98	1,455	0	0	0	0	318
25	26	Belo	Dallas	1,365	1,589	-14.1	1,365	(3)	737		598	0	16	13
26	25	E. W. Scripps	Cincinnati	1,354	1,594	-15.1	1,437	138	739	0	278	0	337	0
27	29	Advo	Windsor, Conn.	1,137	1,129	0.7	1,137	51	0	0	0	0	0	1,137
28	30	Vivendi Universal	New York/Paris	1,119	1,090	2.7	5,285	384	0	0	0	0	1,119	0
29	27	International Data Group	Boston	1,104	1,312	-15.8	3,000	n/a	0	959	0	0	0	145
30	28	McClatchy Co.	Sacramento, Calif.	1,040	1,129	-7.9	1,080	58	1,040	0	0	0	0	0
31	32	Discovery Communications	Bethesda, Md.	985	984	0.1	1,520	n/a	0	0	0	0	985	0
32	33	MediaNews Group	Denver	979	949	3.2	979	25	977	0	3	0	0	0
33	34	Meredith Corp.	Des Moines, Ia.	886	941	-5.8	1,044	71	0	610	270	0	0	6
34	36	Univision Communications	Los Angeles	878	863	1.7	888	52	0	0	872	0	0	6

(continued)

| RANK | | | | TOTAL NET U.S. MEDIA REVENUE | | | | | NET U.S. REVENUE BY MEDIUM, 2001 | | | | | |
2001	2000	Media Company	Headquarters	2001	2000	Percent Change	Worldwide Parent Revenue	Worldwide Net Income	Newspaper	Magazine	TV	Radio	Cable	Other
35	37	Reed Elsevier	London	855	862	−0.8	6,576	(206)	0	855	0	0	0	0
36	39	Valassis Communications	Livonia, Mich.	850	837	1.6	850	118	0	0	0	0	0	850
37	31	McGraw-Hill Cos.	New York	846	990	−14.5	4,646	377	0	741	106	0	0	0
38	41	MediaCom Communications Corp.	Middletown, N.Y.	839	788	6.5	590	(191)	0	0	0	0	839	0
39	40	Media General	Richmond, Va.	809	831	−2.7	807	18	542	0	258	0	0	9
40	42	A&E Television Networks	New York	804	770	4.5	804	n/a	0	18	0	0	786	0
41	38	Reader's Digest Association	Pleasantville, N.Y.	791	843	−6.2	2,369	n/a	0	783	0	0	0	8
42	46	Freedom Communications	Irvine, Calif.	760	734	3.5	760	n/a	663	0	97	0	0	0
43	4	Gemstar-TV Guide International	Pasadena, Calif.	741	739	0.3	1,368	(600)	0	533	0	0	107	101
44	52	Gruner & Jahr (Bertelsmann)	New York/Hamburg, Germany	735	629	16.8	8,592	641	0	735	0	0	0	0

TOTAL NET U.S. MEDIA REVENUE / NET U.S. REVENUE BY MEDIUM, 2001

RANK 2001	RANK 2000	Media Company	Headquarters	2001	2000	Percent Change	Worldwide Parent Revenue	Worldwide Net Income	Newspaper	Magazine	TV	Radio	Cable	Other
45	43	Landmark Communications	Norfolk, Va.	732	757	-3.4	805	n/a	439	0	69	0	224	0
46	48	Lamar Advertising Corp.	Baton Rouge, La.	729	687	6.1	729	(109)	0	0	0	0	0	729
47	50	Lifetime Entertainment Services	New York	727	663	9.7	727	n/a	0	0	0	0	727	0
48	58	Insight Communications Co.	New York	704	476	47.9	704	(94)	0	0	0	0	704	0
49	47	Sinclair Broadcast Group	Hunt Valley, Md.	646	727	-11.1	710	(128)	0	0	646	0	0	0
50	49	Zuckerman Media Properties	New York	613	667	-8.1	n/a	n/a	392	221	0	0	0	0

Note: Dollars are in millions. Media defined as media distribution businesses supported by advertising. Media revenue, considered estimates, are for the latest available fiscal year. Parent returns are as reported; parent revenue may be smaller than media total because media are pro forma where possible and often represent corporate segment totals without eliminations. Figures are an Ad Age analysis of measured media data from Taylor Nelson Sofres' Competitive Media Reporting, BIA Financial Network (radio, TV), Duncan's Radio Market Guide, Paul Kagan Associates (cable), Audit Bureau of Circulations, and public documents.

Source: *Advertising Age*, August 19, 2002, p. S-2.

Uncle Miltie's Lasting Legacy: Advertisers Can't Bank on Re-Creating History

FRED DANZIG

In the late 1940s, Milton Berle's TV show motivated Americans to go out and buy a little black-and-white set so they could watch his raucous vaudeville routines, the seltzer-schpritzing, mugging with blacked-out teeth and manic skits.

Yes, he was usually tasteless and crude. But, hey, the show was live. It was TV. It had yucks. It was better than those B&W test patterns. And it was free.

The death of "Uncle Miltie" last month, at ninety-three, inspired articles about how and why he became our "Mr. Television" but also set in motion attempts to relate his six-year "Texaco Star Theater" run to today's marketing environment. What long-forgotten secrets of Berle's success can be applied to audience building, brand loyalty, and lasting impact in this new century?

The answer: for TV advertisers, few if any.

Berle's success blurs today's marketing vision. Our latest, most ambitious TV deals cannot come close to matching what Berle and his Texaco sponsor accomplished back in TV's pioneering forties and fifties. Yet the Berle era is destined to remain a narrow, primitive model, chiefly because today's marketplace carries enormously higher price tags and more options.

NOT LIKE "THE EARLY DAYS"

Take the latest big deal: Ford Motor Company's agreement to give NBC $9 million worth of network advertising in return for heavy cross-promotional marketing and tie-in marketing programs involving Lincoln vehicles and Jay Leno's "Tonight" audience. It has been described as "reminiscent of the early days of TV, when advertisers unsubtly sponsored entire shows."

Really? Is "Tonight" being renamed "The Lincoln Star Theater"? In "the early days," newly installed TV executives desperately looked to radio for their programming, just as earlier radio executives looked to vaudeville. There were only around 100,000 TV sets in use in January 1948, when Kudner Agency executive vice president Myron Kirk began working on transferring his Texaco-sponsored Berle radio show to TV.

Warning: the following paragraph may cause dizziness and elevated blood pressure among many TV advertisers. Reader discretion is advised.

When "The Texaco Star Theater" officially made its debut on NBC-TV in September 1948, its weekly budget was $15,000. That's not even $1 million for a full thirty-nine-week season. Berle—TV star, director, producer, writer, costumer, makeup man, whatever—received $1,250 per show.

By 1949, however, there were 700,000 home TV sets in use, Berle was up to $6,000 a week, and in TV Land, more Americans were visiting their TV-equipped neighbors' homes to enjoy the show.

During the next two years, 7.4 million more TV sets were added, and major advertisers rushed to attach their names to TV programs. Along came "Hallmark Hall of Fame," "Ford Startime," "DuPont Show of the Month," "GE Theater," "Camel News Caravan," "Bob Hope's Chrysler Theater," "Gillette Cavalcade of Sports," "Kraft Music Hall." Full sponsorship's glory years—with sixty-second commercials—were under way. Of course, during the next ten years, ad costs escalated by 500 percent, and doubled again between 1959 and 1971.

Advertisers, forced to scale back, settled for alternate-week or cosponsorship arrangements, thirty- and ten-second spots, and looked for TV "specials" to get attention. Our Mr. Television, burned out by then, was headlining "Jackpot Bowling."

In 1976, recalling those years, Dick Pinkham, chairman of the Ted Bates & Company executive committee, referred to Uncle Miltie's 8:00 P.M.–to–9:00 P.M. Tuesday hour as TV's "golden time period." The reasons? One advertiser, Texaco, owned the time period, had its name on a show tailored to attract its target audience, enjoyed cost protection, and even had in-show commercials delivered by the star. For a bonus, Mr. Pinkham cited a viewer "gratitude factor," long gone with the advent of the TV scatter buy.

He could have tossed one more bonus onto the pile—Berle's opening jingle: "Oh, we're the men of Texaco/We work from Maine to Mexico/There's nothing like this Texaco of ours . . ."

It's still out there.

NOT EVEN CLOSE

Can any of today's time periods—gold, silver, or bronze—compare? Will the Lincoln-NBC-Leno concerts become a twenty-first-century version of Kudner-Texaco-Berle? Or the modest Dr. Scholl's product placement tie-in with CBS's

"Survivor"? Or any number of major-advertiser ties to seasonal TV specials or sports events?

Not even close.

The point is that Berle's impact will always be a historic curiosity, an incentive, a case history of ultimate TV power. But it's not a realistic advertising goal, given today's media milieu.

Instead, Berle's accomplishment should inspire advertisers to go the non-TV route with customized, well-funded marketing programs linked to all sorts of worthy causes at city, state, regional, or national levels. Creative, serious, long-range tie-ins can generate lasting, Berlean exposure for sponsors. And the cost, relatively, would be more manageable. Throw in that "gratitude factor," and TV's fabled Uncle Miltie impact can yet serve to inspire marketing's next legends, out where blacked-out teeth and outrageous comedy skits aren't the whole story.

Fred Danzig was editor of Advertising Age *for ten of his thirty-three years with that newspaper. He is one of those who would watch Uncle Miltie on a neighbor's TV set. Last year, he and that neighbor's daughter celebrated their fiftieth wedding anniversary. This piece originally appeared as a "Viewpoint" article in the April 22, 2002, issue of* Advertising Age.

CHAPTER 5

THE DILUTION OF CREATIVITY

It's Tougher to Get the Attention of Consumers Swamped with Ad Messages

Perhaps nothing demonstrated the challenges facing the advertising agency business as clearly as an *Advertising Age* headline in mid-2002: "Riney pronounces thirty-second ad dead."

The article referred to Hal Riney, founder and former head of his eponymous agency (since sold to Publicis) and one of the top creative figures of the last thirty years. "After at least two generations of television bombardment in the United States, the magic of traditional advertising is no longer magic," Riney told *Ad Age* reporter Alice Z. Cuneo. The thirty-second television commercial, he added, "is often virtually ineffective."

This statement comes from a man whose television commercials were instrumental in successful campaigns for all kinds of clients, ranging from Saturn cars to Bartles & Jaynes wine coolers to President Ronald Reagan's 1984 reelection. His agency produced memorable work to establish and enhance brand names.

But he realizes that the world has changed, even though many in the advertising business are acting as if it hasn't. Perhaps the most important change that prompted Riney's comment is the proliferation of media, which is treated at length in Chapter 4 of this book.

The impact of television on our consciousness has ebbed. It is not uncommon for people of Baby Boomer age and older to remember television commercials that haven't run for decades. (I can even recite any number of pretelevision *radio* commercials!) Although there is no scientific evidence to support it, I would wager that today's young people will not be able to remember contemporary commercials forty years from now.

The reason for this is obvious: saturation.

Forty years ago, television was a new medium. We watched it with a heightened sense of concentration because it was so new. People described television as being "like movies in your living room." And we watched television that way, in a darkened room, often accompanied by family and friends, especially those who weren't lucky enough to have their own television set. That same level of concentration was applied to commercials. But it didn't last as long. As soon as viewers realized they had seen a particular commercial a dozen or a hundred times, they would head to the bathroom or the refrigerator.

There were commercials that remained memorable, like those for Lite Beer, Hertz car rental, Alka-Seltzer, Timex watches, and others. But just because a commercial is memorable doesn't mean that it was an effective commercial or even that it contained award-winning creative work. What these commercials did was break through the mental filter we raise when our television program has been interrupted. Here's an example of how that happens.

Scene in a crime drama: Police are knocking on the door of an apartment. Nobody answers. They try the doorknob, but it's locked. The officer then steps back and lunges at the door with his shoulder. (Try this, and you'll end up with a broken shoulder.) Inside, we see the body of a nude woman, partially covered by a bloody sheet. The camera zooms in on a knife that has been plunged into her chest.

Cut to commercial: "Hi, I'm John Sincere from the Trustworthy and Honest Insurance Company. Are you sure your insurance is adequate to cover your family's needs if anything were to happen to you? What if you were out of the picture [illustration of a father with his family, but his image disappears]? Can they get along? They can if you have made plans in advance. . . ."

We have all seen these unfortunate juxtapositions of programming with commercials. Today, after having watched hundreds of thousands of commercials in our lives, we have mental filters that are virtually impenetrable. We may see a new commercial and give it a moment or so of attention. If it is engaging, we might spread that attention over two or three viewings. After that, the mental filter automatically gets increasingly difficult to penetrate when we recognize an old commercial. As Hal Riney said, the ad has become virtually ineffective.

Advertising agencies face a three-faceted problem. The first aspect of the problem is that broadcast television advertising is not as important as it was years ago. Broadcast television doesn't have the same coverage as it did in the 1970s. Other media alternatives have chipped away at television's once commanding presence. The second facet is that the concept of advertising itself is not as important as it was years ago. Advertising has lost a considerable amount of influence to other forms of marketing communications, such as sales promotion, public relations, and sponsorship.

These two factors lead me to the third facet of the problem, that the creative aspect of advertising is not as important as it was twenty or thirty years ago. This doesn't mean that creativity isn't still a vital element in advertising, but other factors have become more crucial to the marketing function. When I say creativity is less important, I am referring to the creative function in its most commonly accepted definition, the embodiment of a marketing strategy in the creation of advertising through copywriting, illustration, photography, television production, and so on.

There is a broader definition of creativity that could and should include strategy, positioning, media selection, and other less narrow areas. Most advertising people would agree with this broader definition of creativity. However, when it comes to judging the "creative" output of advertising agencies, all but a handful use the narrower version of creative. The most creative ad agency supposedly is the one that has won the most awards at, say, the International Advertising Festival in Cannes, followed by the Addy Awards, Clio Awards, or any of the other advertising competitions. All of these competitions compare only the craftsmanship of advertising, rather than the results of the advertising. Precious few competitions grant awards based on the effectiveness of the advertising, with the most prominent being the American Marketing Association's Effie awards.

BIGGER IS BLANDER

One of the nuances lost in the massive restructuring of the business into huge holding companies is the personalities of the agencies, which used to be reflected in the creativity of the ads they created. A Doyle Dane Bernbach ad had a distinctively different look from a Leo Burnett ad or a Chiat-Day ad. It is much more difficult today to detect these differences or to see this kind of identifying mark on much of today's advertising.

There are still some small agencies whose personalities show through in their advertising, but this is not as common as it was thirty years ago. As a result, advertising has become more or less homogenized. Thirty years ago, there were some brilliant creative ads. There were also some ads that agencies should have been embarrassed to produce. We have reached a point, however, where most advertising—at least on the national level—is acceptable, maybe even pretty good. Not great, but not terrible, either.

There are reasons for this. Any agency can—and they usually do—pick up ideas and techniques from other agencies. The dissemination of new creative work goes on constantly. New commercials are distributed worldwide via the Internet just hours after they make their debut.

A viewing of commercials from different countries shows that creative ideas are routinely copied or adopted. It used to be that the United States was the creative inspiration for most of the world's advertising business. In recent years, however, exemplary or breakthrough creative is just as likely to come from England, Brazil, or Spain.

Another factor in the rising level of the least-common-denominator status of advertising is technology. A high level of sophisticated computer graphics, for example, is available in every country of the world. It is less expensive, more rapidly produced, and more easily altered than at any time in the past. There is no reason for any agency in any country to produce a commercial or a print ad with inferior production values.

Factors internal to agencies and clients are also contributing to the homogenization of advertising. As opposed to the work produced by creative directors who were also the entrepreneur heads of their agencies during that era of advertising, today's creative work must be approved by review boards of vastly larger agencies and must also get the approval of vastly larger client bureaucracies. The approval often does not come from creative executives, nor even from advertising people, but from business-minded MBAs.

A TOUGHER AUDIENCE

Finally, we must also consider some realities regarding the targets of advertising—us. Those who are making ads are no less creative than their predecessors of years past. But they do have a tougher audience. The majority of consumers in the United States and most other wealthy countries have endured a lifetime of watching television commercials. It is much more difficult today for a commercial to make us laugh or cry, make us cringe in shock or nod in agreement, make us believe in and buy the product being advertised. We have seen it all. We are saturated with advertising. Maybe we have become immune to advertising.

One watershed event in advertising creativity occurred during the 2000 Super Bowl broadcast, when several virtually unknown Internet websites spent upwards of $2 million per commercial to advertise their services. Unfortunately, the advertising was so "creative" that it was impossible in some cases to determine exactly what services the advertiser was offering to the audience. By the time Super Bowl 2001 came around, at least four of the advertisers (Epidemic Marketing, Computer.com, Netpliance, and OnMoney.com) were out of business, perhaps because of irrelevant advertising.

If advertising has become more careful in recent years—which I believe is the case—Super Bowl 2000 was one expensive object lesson in why it has happened. The basic mission of any advertisement—especially for a new product or company—is to disseminate information, something these advertisers did poorly. How can a commercial demonstrate that its product will fulfill a need for consumers when it doesn't say what the product does?

There are other good reasons for advertising to be a little more self-conscious. These range from government regulation to political correctness. Many popular advertisements that appeared in the 1960s would be booed off television today because they showed women in subservient positions or members of ethnic groups in stereotypical or demeaning roles, or perhaps because they made performance claims that couldn't be verified.

A lot of advertising has also become formulated. A few years back, I saw a presentation by an agency creative director that demonstrated quite clearly this notion of the interchangeable television commercial. He would show the first twenty seconds or so of a television commercial, then stop the tape and ask if anyone could tell what product was being advertised. Usually, no one in the audience had a clue. Most of these commercials showed clichéd slice-of-life scenes of children on playground swings, or a young couple diving into a swimming pool, or two handsome older gentlemen smiling and playing checkers. Who was the client? There was virtually no difference between the opening setups, whether for insurance companies, credit cards, cereals, soft drinks, fast-food franchises, or constipation remedies. At one point, the creative director even played a Coca-Cola and a Pepsi-Cola commercial back to back. The only difference from what you may have seen on television is that he put the Coke sound-track on the Pepsi commercial and vice versa. The remarkable demonstration showed that the soundtracks were virtually inter-changeable, as were the accompanying videos.

The growing sameness of advertising has been demonstrated in the various advertising competitions, where the winning entries increasingly are for "ghost ads." These are ads created specifically to enter in competitions, even though they never appeared in the media. In some cases, the agencies may not even represent the clients for whom the ad was created. The entrants are just trying to win an award and get some notoriety for their work. But their envelope-pushing creative can't get client approval.

At the 2001 International Advertising Festival in Cannes, the top creative event of the year, a dozen entries were thrown out for being ghost ads. In some cases, competition winners had to return their trophies after it was determined the ads were fake or perhaps were never aired. The practice of entering ghost ads has become so common that in 2002 the London International Advertising Awards added print, outdoor, and broadcast categories specifically for ghost ads that never ran in the media. The only requirement is that the agencies must actually represent the clients featured in the ads.

Advertising that never ran is often more creative and ground-breaking than advertising that did run. Why? Because it did not have to go through the bureaucratic review process of agencies and clients, which has added to the homogenization of advertising.

None of this means that advertising is any worse or less inviting today than it was in 1960. It has changed, of course. There is less of a gap between the best and the worst advertising. And just as most of today's cars look pretty much the same, so does advertising.

Because of these limitations, blockbuster advertising is much more difficult to create today than it was thirty or forty years ago. It is all the more difficult because many of the broadcast standards imposed on television programming in earlier years have eroded.

Coarse language, overt sexual references, sophomoric dirty jokes, near nudity, and graphic violence in programming are all over cable television. They have also found their way into network television programming. The result is that virtually all commercials seem bland by comparison with the programming.

The proliferation of cable and satellite channels will also affect advertising creativity. With a narrower audience, a commercial can be tailored more closely to the demographics and psychographics of the people watching the program. Marketers should be able to communicate more effectively with these niche audiences because they know more about them. If an advertiser is going to put a spot on the testosterone-injected "The Man Show" on the Comedy Channel, the message can be aimed directly at a male audience, with most viewers probably between twenty and forty years old, and a touch more lecherous or raucous. The creative concept, execution, nuances, and sly signals can be very narrowly targeted to these viewers. A woman might be offended by such a commercial, but she would be offended by the program itself anyway, so the advertiser wouldn't worry about her. The same advertiser might also run on NBC-TV's "Friends," but it would use a different commercial, one that would be more acceptable to a combined male-female audience.

This is the way it should be. The nature of the audience should dictate the creative approach and execution of an advertisement. A commercial on cable's Food Network can be more intense than one for the same product on ABC-TV's "Good Morning America."

GLOBAL ADS? NOT YET

Since we are in an era of global advertisers, global ad agencies, and global media, we might assume that we face a strong future of global advertising campaigns. To some extent, that is true. But with different cultures, languages, mores, demographics, and standards of living, the concept of global advertising is just that, a concept. Very few commercials can run worldwide and be equally effective and accepted without substantial changes.

There could be a global strategy, but the execution and even the media to be used may change from one country to the next. This, of course, is the argument for the global advertising agency that can offer the local orientation for a global product.

※ ※ ※ ※

So here we have a list of subtle and not-so-subtle changes that have taken place in advertising in the last few years. It starts with the consolidation of advertising clout into a few hands. Add to that the decline of advertising's relative importance, the homogenization of creativity, the bureaucracy of big agencies and big clients, and the impact of globalization.

This confluence of trends, it seems to me, explains why the advertising business is more challenging than ever before. It is also more businesslike. Because of that, it has lost much of the glamour, excitement, and fun associated with it during its entrepreneurial years. With advertising dominated by the four publicly owned holding companies, the economic aspects of advertising have overtaken the creative aspects. The pride of authorship has been overtaken by the prospect of profitability.

Agencies still want to produce outstanding work, and clients want to get it, but this is all done with a more disciplined economic approach. In a business sense, the advertising agency business has grown up. It is far more serious. Maybe that's why they don't call it the "ad game" anymore.

Advertising Made Simple: In Times of Cocooning and Comfort Food, Focus on the Basics

STEVE NOVICK

Everyone's mental switchboard is still on overload. People everywhere talk about being distracted, being unable to finish projects, being unable even to sit still. Anxiety and concentration can't coexist. Being nervous, being jittery means being unfocused.

In an increasingly complex world, we're all yearning for simplicity. We're back to simple values: religion, the comfort of friends and family, and the desire to stay home and cocoon.

We're back to simple pleasures: comfort food instead of lavish menus, a bottle of Chianti instead of an overpriced cabernet. Much of what people bragged about two months ago seems tasteless now. Trendy hot spots go empty while neighborhood restaurants are packed.

The implication for advertising is this: We, too, need to get back to what's simple. We need simple ideas, not simplistic ideas. Ideas still need to be big. But more than ever they need to be clear and focused.

WE NEED SIMPLE MESSAGES

In a world where people have trouble focusing, they can't be expected to decipher complicated advertising. No one wants to pay that much attention. No one has the energy. Don't expect people to work so hard; they're not going to be studying our ads.

Here are a few of the old rules that are even truer now:

* A spot can have only one idea, not three, and one benefit, not a multilayered offering.
* The days of the complex "reason why" are over. People cannot be argued into buying a product.
* The more words you use, the more counterproductive your effort. Tell me once, or better yet, just show me.

HUMOR, PLEASE!

If there was ever a time when advertising and entertainment needed to converge, it's now. People are hungry for a moment of relief, a little island of pleasure that will offer respite from the day's news. With their "worst nightmare" on their minds, we need to entertain to break through. Ads that entertain are like oxygen: a moment to breathe, a release from the events of the day.

Laughter is the ultimate escape from stress. But the kind of humor that's appropriate has changed. We've already observed that snide, cynical humor no longer resonates.

* Poking fun is still fine, but disparagement is not.
* Forced humor—jokes that are stiff and artificial—always fell flat. That hasn't changed at all. It's now more inappropriate than ever.
* Stupid humor, the "dumbing down" of America, is passé. People are proving every day that they can deal with weighty issues. Humor that treats people like adolescents is condescending unless, of course, they are adolescents.

One kind of humor that will resonate is what I call "behavioral humor." It's humor that comes from a witty observation about the little things that people do. It comes out of the unaffected remarks that kids make and the natural way they behave. It finds charm in people's little human foibles and idiosyncrasies. It pokes fun at classic patterns of behavior. We can identify with that. It's real, it's genuine, and it's not unkind. It makes us feel good. It lifts us.

PRODUCTS CAN'T BE HEROES; PEOPLE ARE

"Make the product the hero" is an old expression that's not right today. The product can play a role in allowing a person to be a hero, but the product itself probably isn't heroic, and it shouldn't be portrayed that way.

Don't exaggerate. Products can't be the focus of our attention because they're not enough to hold our attention. It's the way people interact with products, the way they behave, that makes a story engaging.

The audience will identify with a moment of human triumph. People long for stories they can identify with—small achievements, where an obstacle is overcome or a person does something surprising.

Make sure the brand is modest if it takes some of the credit. Don't expect people to worship the goods. People want to connect with somebody, not something.

WATCH THE FLAG-WAVING

An idea doesn't get better because it's draped in the flag. We've come to appreciate the flag more than ever since September 11, but this is a time to use it judiciously.

Of course, there are brands whose heritage is connected to the flag (from the U.S. Postal Service to Tommy Hilfiger).

But heritage is one thing; climbing on the flag-waving band-wagon is another. Pseudo-patriotism is barely veiled profiteering, and it is not going to resonate with the American consumer. It's a callous sale.

TRUST THE IDEA; DON'T OVERPRODUCE IT

An overproduced piece of advertising is the antithesis of what we need now. Overproduction just overcomplicates.

Injecting money and techniques that are supposed to make an ad more interesting only makes it more expensive. That just brings conspicuous consumption to the TV screen.

Of course, simple ideas must be engaging and entertaining and well executed. But that doesn't require self-indulgence or lavishness. Watching Willie Nelson singing "America the Beautiful" can be more electrifying, and more appropriate, than a chorus of 100.

"Simple" may look easy, but it isn't easy. Simplicity exposes the quality of an idea. Although we may have become accustomed to overthinking and overproducing, now is the time to simplify.

Steve Novick is vice chairman–chief creative officer of Grey Global Group, New York. This piece was originally published as an article in Advertising Age's *November 12, 2001, "Forum" section.*

CHAPTER 6

THERE IS NO LINE

Once-Scorned Alternatives Gain Respect and a Bigger Piece of the Marketing Pie

Back in 2000, I was invited by a Polish advertising organization to give a speech in Warsaw on trends in the business. Having put together a considerable amount of detail on the topic, I agreed to do it. It also gave me an opportunity to do some other business in Eastern Europe and visit *Advertising Age*'s licensees in that region. As we communicated by E-mail, my hosts made a request that made me shake my head.

"Please," they asked, "could you please talk only about ATL? We don't want to hear anything about BTL. We want to know how we can fight against BTL."

It took me a minute to understand what they were looking for. This group wanted me to address my remarks only to "above-the-line" advertising, which is traditional advertising placed on the major media: newspapers, television, magazines, radio, and out-of-home. These functions produced revenues in the old days. Everything else was an expense and was below the revenue line. My hosts didn't want me to mention "below-the-line" activities because these marketing activities were threatening the traditional advertising business. Because communism considered advertising to be evil, its development was stunted for many years in Eastern Europe. They hadn't caught up with the global trends and they felt threatened by new forms of advertising.

In replying to their request, I told my hosts that I could not talk about trends in advertising without talking about the growth in below-the-line marketing. "In fact," I suggested, "The title of my talk will be, 'There Is No Line.'" They were very gracious in acquiescing to my suggestion, and the speech went over well with the audience, although there might have been some grumbling in the back rows.

I learned as much from my hosts as they learned from me. The first factor to understand is that advertising in Poland and the other former Soviet Bloc countries was largely prohibited until the Iron Curtain crumbled in 1991. Poland's advertising industry was quite new then. The business included affiliates of many of the major global agencies, as well as a sprinkling of local agencies headed by spirited entrepreneurs. For the first time in their lives, these people could openly practice capitalism. They could watch commercial television and see magazines with ads for products that a few years earlier existed only in their fantasies.

Advertising to them, however, was not only a way to build brands and sell products, it also gave them an opportunity to make public pronouncements in the media. They were exercising their long-sought freedom of speech, although in many countries it is still not as free as it is in the United States.

Traditional advertising was still growing in Poland, largely because of the growth in media not controlled by the government. But even then, many clients were using other forms of marketing. They were into below-the-line because it was the most efficient way of selling their products and services.

The essence of my talk in Poland was similar to what you have been reading in this book. It is that advertising is changing, and it is changing very rapidly. One of those dramatic changes is the growth of many forms of new and old marketing that are lumped together under the "below-the-line" banner. In my opinion, there is no longer the need for any "line" to mark the difference between traditional media advertising and other forms of reaching consumers. Since advertising practitioners no longer rely on media commissions as their sole source of revenues, there is no reason for them not to embrace whatever tactic it takes to build brands and sell products. And this situation should prevail across the globe, including the United States.

In this country, direct-marketing and sales promotion activities by advertising agencies in 2001 yielded them $5.32 billion in revenues. Advertising services produced $14.1 billion in revenues (*Advertising Age*, May 20, 2002). This is an interesting comparison, considering that most of these agencies only recently established major presences in these nonadvertising fields.

To me, the most important aspect of below-the-line marketing for ad agency people is that it gives them a broader array of tools with which to fashion a successful marketing campaign for a client. It gives them the ultimate freedom of creativity. They no longer have to be shackled by the print ad, radio commercial, or television spot.

It would take an encyclopedia to list all of the forms of alternative marketing available to clients. I will try to cover some of the more important areas in the following paragraphs.

DIRECT MARKETING

To some extent, Chapter 3 has already covered direct marketing, but it is important to recognize the size and impact of this industry. Research conducted by the Wharton Economic Forecasting Associates for the Direct Marketing Association reports that direct marketing expenditures in 2001 were $196.8 billion, up 3.6 percent from the previous year. This figure includes Internet interactive advertising.

This gain took place even though the advertising business was suffering through its worst year-to-year drop in spending in more than sixty years. More importantly, the report estimates that direct marketing generated $1.86 trillion in sales in 2001. For the future, direct-marketing expenditures are expected to rise at an annual rate of 6.5 percent until 2006. At the same time, sales are projected to grow 8.5 percent a year, indicating increased productivity for the marketing discipline. (There is a considerable discrepancy between *Advertising Age* figures and those from the DMA. That is because the DMA figures include direct spending by clients, while *Ad Age* counts only revenues derived by outside agencies.)

One of the key reasons clients have shifted larger budgets into direct marketing is that it is directly accountable. A client can determine the return on investment from a particular campaign or effort. This is not easily or accurately calculated in the use of traditional media advertising.

A development that fueled the growth in direct marketing was the evolution of the Internet into a direct-response medium. At the moment of the World Wide Web's inception in 1994, direct marketers realized the potential of the Internet as an effective way to reach potential customers. A 1998 report from Andersen Consulting (now Accenture) asserts, "Many traditional ad firms still tend to view the Internet as just another passive ad medium, rather than a powerful, two-way channel for learning about, and marketing to, consumers."

To Howard Draft, chairman of Interpublic's Draft Worldwide, "the Internet is not that important yet . . . but it is growing in importance and it is a strong loyalty tool." He says loyalty building is a primary and effective function of direct marketing, even though direct marketing isn't as effective in initiating loyalty.

Draft Worldwide, one of the largest direct-marketing firms in the world, generated about $381 million in 2001 revenues through sixty offices, according to *Advertising Age*. Draft describes the company as a "fully integrated marketing company," producing all services except media advertising. Of the top ten direct-marketing agencies in the United States, five are owned by the major holding companies and two are owned by other advertising agencies.

Although direct marketing has never commanded the media attention of advertising (after all, direct marketing competes with print, for example), it gained a new level of stature in 2002. That was the first year that the International Advertising Festival in Cannes added a direct-marketing category and presented its Lion awards to winning entrants.

Table 6.1 describes the top ten direct-marketing agencies in the United States.

TABLE 6.1	TOP TEN DIRECT-MARKETING AGENCIES, RANKED BY U.S. REVENUE FROM DIRECT MARKETING					
RANK				**U.S. DIRECT-MARKETING REVENUE**		
2001	**2000**	**Agency** (Parent [Network])	**Head-quarters**	**2001**	**2000**	**% Change**
1	2	DraftWorldwide (Interpublic [Lowe])	Chicago	$240.9	$251.5	−4.2
2	1	Digitas	Boston	235.5	288.2	−18.3
3	3	Rapp Collins Worldwide (Omnicom)	New York	202.2	216.0	−6.3
4	4	Wunderman (WPP [Y&R])	New York	173.0	197.0	−12.1
5	5	OgilvyOne Worldwide (WPP [O&M])	New York	169.6	173.5	−2.2
6	6	Aspen Marketing Group	Los Angeles	109.9	156.2	−29.7
7	7	TMP Worldwide	New York	106.0	109.0	−2.7
8	8	MRM Partners (Interpublic [McCann])	New York	106.0	107.0	−0.9
9	9	Brann Worldwide (Havas [Arnold])	Wilton, Conn.	98.6	103.3	−4.5
10	10	Grey Direct Marketing Group (Grey Global)	New York	88.0	80.0	10

Note: Dollars are in millions. Rank for 2000 is based on data reported to *Ad Age* in 2002.
Source: *Advertising Age*, April 22, 2002, p. S-14.

SALES PROMOTION

The area of sales promotion includes a large variety of services whose aim is to help a company's sales force get a product into the wholesale and retail distribution chain and then promote sales to the final customer. As the next chapter points out in discussing retailing, getting a new product on the shelves of a supermarket chain is not a slam dunk, even for the biggest packaged-goods companies in the world. One common way to help in this process is by employing trade promotions with wholesalers and retailers. These might include discounts and rebates, promotional allowances, contributions to a retailer's advertising budget, in-store displays, and tie-ins with more established products. And, of course, there is always the slotting allowance that most clients have to pay to get their new products into the distribution channel.

If distribution is accomplished, marketers then might employ a variety of consumer-targeted sales promotion techniques such as in-store sampling, coupons, premium giveaways, shelf talkers, contests, sweepstakes, cobranding with other products, and all kinds of collateral material. If advertising is associated with a sales promotion, the advertising is usually created specifically for the promotion and is often produced by the promotion company rather than the advertising agency.

Bud Frankel, founder and chairman emeritus of Frankel & Company, one of the industry's leading firms, maintains that "most ad agencies just don't understand sales promotion," especially the multilevel function of promoting to the wholesale, retail, and consumer levels at the same time. "Without that distribution, you aren't going to sell your products, no matter what kind of advertising you have."

Frankel comes to this conclusion with a background of forty years in the business and a client list that includes companies like

McDonald's, United Airlines, Target, and Nestlé. He also maintains that sales promotion has always accounted for at least 50 percent of marketing budgets but has never been accurately counted. One reason is that most lists and reports count only the work done by outside companies like Frankel. They usually do not include the sales promotion work done internally by a client company.

One other point Frankel's long experience illustrates is the growing maturity of the sales promotion industry. When he started in the business in 1962, sales promotion companies usually charged no specific fees, but generated revenues by marking up the cost of materials produced for their clients. It's all more formalized now. Promotion companies typically charge fees for their work and usually operate under a contract.

Giving evidence of the acquisitive nature of the major advertising holding companies—and their desire to diversify—Frankel & Company was acquired by Publicis in 2000.

Sometimes advertising has to compete against sales promotion for a client's marketing dollars. One example involves H. J. Heinz Company, which has shifted its strategies over the years from one discipline to the other. In 1994 the company severed its thirty-six-year relationship with Leo Burnett Company because it had decided to use "nontraditional marketing—targeted marketing and micromarketing" for its brands such as Star-Kist tuna and 9-Lives cat food. The company has since altered its spending patterns, but promotion remains an important element in its strategy.

PUBLIC RELATIONS

The marketing discipline of public relations dates back to the advance man for the circus. PR has finally started attracting some deserved attention in recent years. In fact, it got more than it deserved in a controversial book written in 2002 by Al and Laura Ries, *The Fall of Advertising and the Rise of PR* (HarperCollins).

The Rieses (father and daughter) contend that public relations is a more powerful tool than advertising in introducing new products and building brands. Advertising, they write, is better suited for maintaining and defending established brands. The book's title is a vast overstatement, but it is the kind of title that generates publicity and may well boost sales. Al Ries has always been good at that.

Of course, public relations isn't about to replace advertising. There are several reasons. One involves the nature of the product or service being introduced. Something that is truly a breakthrough product, like Viagra, or a product with strong celebrity appeal, like *O, the Oprah Magazine*, provides ready-made opportunities for widespread publicity. Any of the early-morning news-talk shows would love to have the first interview of the developer of Viagra. And they would leap at the chance to go one-on-one with Oprah Winfrey, even if her popular talk show is on a different network.

But most new products and services are pretty mundane. A new brand of frozen broccoli. A new telephone company pricing offer. A new and improved gasoline additive. It is pretty tough to get the attention of a television program manager or a newspaper managing editor with stuff like that.

Having said that, however, I should add that it is not impossible for a clever PR person to stage a publicity stunt to promote a product that doesn't have inherent public interest. A PR genius could always hire former president George Bush, a renowned broccoli hater, and have him eat some of her client's broccoli on the "Late Show with Dave Letterman." It would get a lot of publicity for a day or two, but then the client would be left with the prospect of somehow persuading the key audience to try the product or, more importantly, persuading the head buyers of the nation's largest supermarket chains to stock it.

Table 6.2, a list of the world's top public relations firms, illustrates the interest of the four major holding companies in this business.

There is a difference between a one-time publicity stunt and a lasting public relations program. Years ago, when I was writing a marketing column for the old *Chicago Daily News*, a publicist came in with a hot-pants-clad model in tow. They were promoting a new razor, and she was going to shave me while a photographer took pictures. Since I had already shaved, she only pretended to shave me while I flirted with her and the photographer snapped away. This was not an unpleasant experience. I still have a copy of that photo, but there was never any publicity in the paper. And I can't even remember what company was involved.

On the other hand, McDonald's Corporation is a great example of a company that has excelled at consistent public relations. Its "spokesclown," Ronald McDonald, is known worldwide and has generated good feelings for the company for decades. This is true for adults as well as children. I have seen him marching in patriotic parades, presiding at restaurant openings, and handing out coupons for free french fries at picnics. The Ronald character has developed into a strong community relations figure.

There is also a very direct and positive connection with Ronald McDonald House Charities, which operates 212 lodging facilities around the world. This program allows families of seriously ill children getting hospital treatment to stay in comfortable quarters nearby for next to nothing. Getting positive public relations from a community program like this is invaluable.

On the more popular side, the hamburger chain has attracted all kinds of attention and business through such promotions as Teenie Beanie Babies and Star Trek merchandise. All of these promotions generate solid public relations, especially when a secondary market for Beanie Babies erupts and generates additional exposure.

TABLE 6.2	TOP FIFTEEN PUBLIC RELATIONS AGENCIES, RANKED BY 2001 WORLDWIDE FEE INCOME

RANK				WORLDWIDE FEE INCOME		
2001	2000	Agency	Parent Ad Organization	2001	2000	% Change
1	1	Weber Shandwick Worldwide	Interpublic Group of Cos.	$426.6	$507.4	−15.9
2	2	Fleishman-Hillard	Omnicom Group	345.1	338.4	2.0
3	4	Hill & Knowlton	WPP Group	325.1	302.8	7.4
4	3	Burson Marsteller*	WPP Group	290.7	334.3	−13.0
5	5	Incepta	Incepta Group	266.0	243.9	9.1
6	6	Edelman Public Relations Worldwide	Independent	223.7	233.4	−4.2
7	7	Porter Novelli*	Omnicom Group	186.3	192.9	−3.4
8	9	Ketchum	Omnicom Group	185.2	168.2	10.1
9	10	GCI Group/APCO Worldwide	Grey Global Group	151.1	150.7	0.3
10	8	Ogilvy Public Relations Worldwide	WPP Group	145.9	169.5	−13.9
11	13	Euro RSCG Corporate Communications	Havas Advertising	124.2	108.0	15.0
12	12	Manning Selvage & Lee	Publicis Groupe (Bcom3 Group)	116.0	118.8	−2.4
13	11	Golin/Harris International	Interpublic Group of Cos.	113.2	134.7	−15.9
14	16	Cordiant Communications Group	Cordiant Communications Group	90.7	79.8	13.6
15	14	Ruder Finn Group	Independent	80.3	84.1	−4.5

*Updated figures supplied by parent.
Note: Dollars are in millions.
Source: Data derived by the Council of Public Relations Firms; published in *Advertising Age*, April 22, 2002, p. S-14.

When one examines the nature of public relations, it is easy to see that this is one of the most adaptable forms of marketing. It can be used in conjunction with media advertising, sponsorship, or sales promotion. Many of McDonald's promotional campaigns are tied to public relations. "Public relations is also very much a part of event marketing," asserts Tom Harris, a public relations consultant and author with a broad background in all forms of public relations, including that for advertising agencies.

While the proliferation of media has created a tougher challenge for advertising agencies, it has opened up tremendous opportunities for those in public relations. "In the old days, we had three networks and three weekly newsmagazines. Now PR people have a lot of media options," Harris says. With the narrower focus of the cable and satellite channels, publicists can arrange for longer-form interviews on specialized programming. The public relations executive of a company that makes fishing rods or lures has a dozen or more outdoor programs on which to get exposure for products or company executives. There were almost no prospects on broadcast television before cable.

Some of this arises from the economics of narrowcasting. Cable networks don't spend as much on production as the broadcast networks do, and interview programs are generally inexpensive to produce. This creates a bonanza for the PR person who has authors, celebrities, or others looking for exposure. The interview opportunities run the gamut from Pat Robertson's "700 Club" to "The Howard Stern Show" and "Live with Regis and Kelly" to "The News-Hour with Jim Lehrer." Cable generally provides more programming about business, health care, personal finance, sports, self-fulfillment, and many other topics. Radio also has opened up substantially for public relations, with so many talk shows on virtually any subject. There also are far more magazines covering special interests or aimed at special audiences, all of which will add up to more interview opportunities.

Because of these factors, public relations has grown in importance in the last few years. The discipline does provide an effective way for some companies and some products to develop a strong brand image. Ben & Jerry's ice cream and Tom's of Maine toothpaste are examples of companies that have developed brand images with virtually no advertising.

Public relations also works well with media advertising, Tom Harris asserts, pointing out that the popular "Whassup" campaign was a big PR winner for Budweiser beer. The young men in the commercials became instant celebrities, appearing on network talk shows and variety programs. In this case, the advertising was driving the public relations, rather than vice versa.

Public relations is also one of the most important elements in customer relationship management (CRM), as well as the loyalty programs run by hotels, airlines, and other retail operations. This function of public relations is far more substantial than merely getting column mentions and sound bites. It means helping build a solid and positive image in the minds of customers, media, legislators, and any other group that is important to the client. This is also a crucial element in developing brand loyalty.

Public relations should really permeate every area in which the public has contact with the client. A CEO's positive interview on "Good Morning America" can be squandered if counter clerks are rude or dismissive or if customers are never able to reach a living human being while trying to call into the company.

The advertising holding companies also understand the importance of public relations. That is why nine of the ten largest public relations firms in the world are owned by the holding companies. Edelman Public Relations Worldwide is the only independent firm in that group.

SPONSORSHIP

We have been inundated with a rapid growth of sponsorship messages in recent years, and this trend isn't going to go away. Every kind of event, from rock concerts to operas, marketing conferences to medical conventions, is financed at least in part by sponsors trying to attract the attention and business of attendees. But these are only the day-to-day demonstrations of the ubiquity of sponsorships.

There are also big-time deals aimed at the broader audience. Take one of the most venerated sports traditions in the United States, the college football bowl games. About twenty-five or so of these bowl games are played every year, and virtually every one of them has a sponsor that paid for the privilege of attaching its name to the game. This is how we ended up with such seemingly incongruous names as the Tostitos Fiesta Bowl, Chick-fil-A Peach Bowl, Wells Fargo Sun Bowl, and Nokia Sugar Bowl. The one holdout so far has been the Rose Bowl, which will not sell its name to the highest bidder . . . well, sort of. The legendary game most recently has been officially identified as ". . . the Rose Bowl, presented by AT&T."

The reasons for such sponsorship are many. Perhaps the most obvious is the exposure that the sponsors will get in every newspaper, magazine, radio, and television story about the bowl game. Then there is the exposure on the game telecast itself, plus the contact with the thousands of fans attending the game. There is also the sponsor's ability to use the game to entertain special clients.

If this exposure is accompanied by some commercials on the telecast of the game, it creates an integrated package that connects the sponsor with an American tradition, generating all kinds of warm vibes. If you take the benefits of being sponsors along with the broadcast rights of whatever television or cable network is airing the game, you can see that these commercial interests "own" these games, even dictating on what day and at what hour the games will be played. The college conferences and tournaments presenting the games don't like to hear this, but it is the only realistic way to look at these relations.

Sports and sponsorships have been tied together for years. That is a good thing for fans, because it is the sponsors that finance the extensive schedule of professional and college sports on television and radio. But the sponsors in recent years have gotten even more involved with another aspect of sports: real estate. For example, there are about 110 professional sports stadiums and arenas in North America. More than half of them now have name sponsors. These range from the Molson Centre in Montreal and Safeco Field in Seattle to the Great Western Forum in Los Angeles and Comerica Park in Detroit.

In addition to the media exposure, there are certain other, perhaps more concrete, benefits a sponsor can derive from the relationship. Pepsi-Cola's sponsorship of the Pepsi Center in Denver provides a good example. As part of the $68 million, fifteen-year deal, Pepsi is the only soft drink sold in the home arena for the National Basketball Association's Denver Nuggets and the National Hockey League's Colorado Avalanche. Pepsico's Frito-Lay, Tropicana, and Quaker Oats products also have first rights to be sold exclusively in the arena.

The amount of Pepsi-Cola sold in the Pepsi Center is not as important as the number of dyed-in-the-wool Coca-Cola drinkers who are forced to shift brands while watching a sports or entertainment event in the arena. In contrast, consider the Michael Jackson concert tour of the 1980s, which Pepsi-Cola paid millions to sponsor. When I attended the concert, there was not a single mention of Pepsi during the program, and Coca-Cola was the only soft drink available at the old Rosemont Horizon (now the Allstate Arena). Pepsi's name was printed on the back of the tickets.

The same principle applies to other products as well. At Miller Park in Milwaukee, fans can buy only one brand of beer (guess which one) while watching a Milwaukee Brewers baseball game. Naming sponsors usually get internal signage in the stadiums, skybox rights, credit in the program books and scorecards, and the ability to conduct sales promotion events with the sports team.

Naming-rights deals, of course, do not always work out the way they were intended. The Houston Astros, for example, no longer play in Enron Field. Having the naming rights to the stadium couldn't counteract the tremendous negative publicity generated when the Enron scandal erupted in 2001. The stadium was simply called Astros Park for a short time, but by mid-2002, the field was renamed Minute Maid Park. As you might have guessed, that's the only brand of orange juice you'll be able to buy there, along with a certain soft drink from Minute Maid's parent company, Coca-Cola Company.

This was not the only sponsorship debacle of recent vintage. Marketing executives went scurrying when legal and financial problems put a cloud over the MCI Center in Washington, D.C., and the Adelphia Coliseum in Nashville, Tennessee. In August 2002, another questionable deal was resolved when Internet conglomerate CMGI Inc. pulled out of its agreement to buy the naming rights to the New England Patriots stadium in Foxboro, Massachusetts. That's probably a good thing, since "CMGI Field" somehow doesn't have a very poetic ring to it.

Naming rights to public venues are not limited to sports arenas. Advertisers are also putting their names on theaters, establishing long-term relationships with venues that would attract good prospects for their products and services. In 2000, American Airlines made a sizable contribution to New York's Roundabout Theatre Company, which allowed the organization to find a permanent home in Times Square. As a result, what used to be the historic Selwyn Theatre was renamed the American Airlines Theatre.

This isn't an isolated example of advertisers coming up with funding to have their names attached to highly visible public venues. In Chicago, for example, car manufacturers seem to have caught on to the idea. That's where we find the Cadillac Palace Theater competing with the Oriental Theater/Ford Center for the Performing Arts, only a block apart from each other in the city's Loop.

In many cases, advertisers may be using funds normally committed to community relations or charitable giving. The association with affluent audiences yields all kinds of marketing benefits.

Don't Rush to Show Biz Deals: Understanding How to Harness the Power of Entertainment

PHIL GUARASCIO

Now that the Screen Actors Guild has tentatively agreed to allow ad agencies or their parent companies to make equity investments in talent agencies, is a flurry of deals likely? Not so fast, please. Let's take a deep breath on the subject of entertainment marketing—or what's better characterized as "marketing through entertainment." It's a paradigm we pioneered at General Motors Corporation more than ten years ago.

Given the attention and ambiguity surrounding this marketing hot button, taking a breath is not a bad thought. There's been lots of speculation about "big deals," joint ventures and acquisitions, but the reality is that both industries, marketing and entertainment, are just beginning to understand how to harness and leverage the power of entertainment as a marketing tool. Further, the suspected deals between the major talent agencies and advertising/marketing companies seem to be just, well, suspect.

This is only a temporary condition, however. There's a growing acceptance of the power of entertainment as a sustaining marketing tool when it's conducted more professionally and in a bigger way. Still, there are a number of issues that need to be addressed before marketing through entertainment can get to this next level.

First, marketers and talent agencies need to understand they share one strong, common bond: They both make their living managing brands. For the talent agency, it might be an author or an actor—but it's a brand, nevertheless. While talent agency methods may be more subjective than those used on Madison Avenue, both want the same end result: a strong, uniquely positioned brand worth a premium to the consumer.

NO REPLACING TALENT AGENCIES

The advertising business needs to recognize talent agencies are the main portal to the entertainment business, and they won't be replaced by ad agencies. On the other hand, ad agencies "own" the client relationship and brand stewardship. While this line may sometimes blur, it can't move.

Having seen both businesses from the inside, there are a lot more differences than appear on the surface. Talent agents exist in a world driven by broad, upstream entertainment knowledge and deal making. They can be superb at creating brand content in an entertainment context. The ad agency's processes are far more disciplined and strategic, and their ability to bring clients to a deal is critical. Here are other key issues:

* Marketing through entertainment needs to be viewed as a strategic, needs-based tool and not a limited tactical weapon. Measurement needs to be created to enable a more fact-based understanding of value. Clients, who pay the bills, need to see it this way.
* The sector is broader than product placement in films and TV. It is the entire world of entertainment platforms: music, theater, digital media, publishing, place-based media, and on and on. In other words, it's about con-

necting brands and people any place, any way, and any time.

* Entertainment initiatives should be leverageable and translatable across platforms and geography.
* A process and champion to nurture entertainment initiatives through ad agency and client organizations will be required because, at this point, these ideas have no natural home at most companies.

As both parties come together on these key points, the major deals will be pursued more realistically. However, there will be financial issues. The talent agency business is essentially a fee-for-services model. It's not obvious that there's enough revenue available relative to the risk to be attractive to the big public holding companies.

Further, ownership of a talent agency isn't required to develop a "first look" arrangement; the ad agencies' ability to bring clients to the table, or a willingness to use media-buying clout to help create distribution, is sufficient inducement.

The issue on the talent agency side is that, in their risk-taking, fast-moving, transaction-oriented world, a relationship with an ad agency could slow them down and make them potentially less attractive to the very talent that is their lifeblood. If talent agencies can own bigger shares in content, particularly in TV shows, as the tentative SAG pact would allow, the model changes. This could easily increase the upside of a holding company investment in a talent agency because content ownership is where the big money lies—and also the bigger risk.

Until this happens, the talent agency is still a fee-for-services business in Hollywood. The main opportunity for advertising agencies is in bringing value-added services to clients and gaining revenue opportunities, through their participation in the execution that grows out of entertainment-based ideas.

The blending of these two businesses under a new model is inevitable. But it will be built on solid business and marketing principles, where clients need to come first.

Phil Guarascio is chairman of PG Ventures, Detroit, a media and marketing company, and former vice president of corporate advertising and marketing, General Motors Corporation. He recently was a consultant for the William Morris Agency, whose clients include GM. This piece originally appeared as a "Viewpoint" article in the March 4, 2002, issue of Advertising Age.

RETAILERS FLEX THEIR MUSCLES

Consolidation in the Retail Sector Imposes Pressure on Everyone in the Marketing Chain

The amount of influence the retail sector exerts on the advertising industry is often underestimated or ignored. But it is there, it is real, and it is growing.

One reason for the growth is the concentration of retailing power in only a few hands. This is most evident in the grocery business, where there are thousands of products with national advertising budgets. Consider that the top three supermarket chains—Kroger, Albertson's, and Safeway—operate a total of 6,500 stores in the United States and rang up some $122 billion in business in 2001. Although you might not have these specific retailer brands in your market, remember that in this age of consolidation, Kroger also owns fifteen other supermarket chains (including Ralph's), 789 convenience stores under six other banners, two food warehouse stores, two department stores, and 437 jewelry stores. What was once a business dominated by locally owned and operated food chains has evolved into a network of behemoths dominated by a few major chains with major regional distribution.

There is an immutable truth in the connection between advertising and the sales of packaged goods: *if you can't get the product on the shelves, all the advertising in the world isn't going to produce any sales.*

This is where the problem lies for packaged-goods marketers. A steady stream of new products flows into the marketplace every year, but there isn't a proportionate increase in the amount of shelf space in the average supermarket. With more products chasing a constant amount of shelf space, it becomes obvious that manufacturers must first persuade wholesalers and retailers to carry their products before they can persuade consumers to buy them.

Twenty-five years ago, a major packaged-goods company would normally launch a new product with a huge advertising campaign, often coupled with a retail promotion campaign. But the advertising was the key to the packaged-goods companies' marketing. The advantage to the retailer was that the manufacturer was going to spend millions of dollars advertising the product, which would drive consumers into the local chain.

Today, any marketer trying to place a new product into retail distribution has to provide an incentive for retail store chains to take on the product. The most common incentive is called a "slotting allowance," giving the product a slot in a distribution chain that is already jammed with entries. And there is a never-ending lineup of other new products that are trying to find their way onto supermarket shelves.

Retail chains monitor the sales records of these new products because they don't want to waste valuable shelf space on items that don't move. The retailer is interested in this kind of information because it enables efficient inventory control and aids in category management, the mantra of the supermarket business. The goal of all retailers is to maximize the profitability from every inch of shelf space and in every product category, mainly because the margin in the food business is lower than in most other industries. Aside from that, the collection of data can also provide an intimate look into the buying habits of individual customers.

Some major manufacturers deny they pay slotting allowances to any supermarket chains, but experts say they usually substitute some other kind of trade promotion allowance in place of the slotting fee. At least one retail and distribution expert feels that manufacturers also have a problem because in recent years they have not produced the kind of breakthrough new products retailers are interested in. "If you consider the disposable diaper as a new product, it was a home run," asserts Eric Strobel, a managing partner in the Partnering Group and a former marketing executive at Kraft Foods and Procter & Gamble. "But what you have now are mainly variations on existing products, different flavors, new packaging and sizes, low-calorie versions. These are singles—bunt singles—not home runs." In effect, they are not revolutionary, breakthrough products for a supermarket. The stores have to be sweet-talked into putting the new product on the shelf, and the sweetest talk a retailer can hear is a slotting allowance or other kind of financial inducement.

In discussing the biggest retail chains, we have omitted Wal-Mart Stores, which actually sells more supermarket merchandise (about $80 billion annually) than any pure supermarket chain. But since supermarket merchandise is only part of the mammoth retailer's $220 billion in annual sales, Wal-Mart is not considered a primary food retailer. Based on sales volume, Wal-Mart is the largest U.S. corporation on the *Fortune* 500 list. (It is also the largest global corporation, having surpassed Exxon Mobil in 2002.) It definitely is a player in the food business, although it may not play by traditional food-retailing rules.

In fact, *Advertising Age* reported that Wal-Mart has become a champion of new products because it doesn't (so far) ask for slotting fees. "Wal-Mart is the first one to get our products because we don't have to pay slotting fees, and if the product is a home run there, other retailers may be willing to bypass slotting fees," Tim McMahon, senior VP, marketing and communications, for ConAgra Foods, told *Ad Age* (*Advertising Age*, April 29, 2002).

That is not likely to happen because retailers are still faced with too many products for the amount of space available. Nevertheless, Wal-Mart has its eye on increasing its share of food retailing, not only through its branded stores, but also through its Sam's Club locations. As more products vie for shelf space, retailers inevitably will demand some kind of concessions from manufacturers, whether they are slotting allowances or other kinds of inducements.

SUPERMARKETS CROSS BORDERS

Along with the concentration of power in the hands of a few operators, what may be another trend in food retailing is the growing internationalization of the supermarket business. Wal-Mart has moved rapidly into that field. It went international in 1991, with locations in Mexico, and has expanded to nine countries with more than 1,000 stores.

Even more international is Royal Ahold, based in the Netherlands. It is the fourth largest food retailer in the United States, with more than $23 billion in business in 2001 through its Stop & Shop, Giant, and other local chains. In all, the company operates nine thousand stores in twenty-eight countries. Ahold has also acquired Peapod, the service through which consumers can order groceries over the Internet and have them delivered to their homes or offices at a specified time.

Another major international player is the France-based Carrefour chain, which operates 9,200 stores in thirty countries, although none in the United States. No one can say how long it will take Carrefour to identify a U.S. acquisition target and move into the world's richest marketplace, but chances are it will happen. That will continue to add to the consolidation trend and the growing power of the retail sector.

An analysis of global retailers compiled by Deloitte Touche Tohmatsu indicates that several European retailers are further along in the international arena than any U.S. retailer, except perhaps for McDonald's. The top fifty global retailers, listed in Table 7.1, include thirteen European and Japanese retailers marketing in at least eleven countries and on more than one continent. Toys "R" Us is the only U.S. retailer with stores in twenty-nine countries and on every continent except Latin America.

Most of the international growth of retailing has come in recent years. It is certainly going to continue in the future.

TABLE 7.1 TOP FIFTY GLOBAL RETAILERS

Deloitte & Touche Rank	Country of Origin	Name of Company	Formats	2001 Sales[a] (in millions of U.S. dollars)	2001 Retail Sales (in millions of U.S. dollars)	2001 Group Income (Loss)[a] (in millions of U.S. dollars)	Countries of Operation
1	U.S.	Wal-Mart	Discount, hypermarket, supermarket, superstore, warehouse	219,812	217,799	6,671	Argentina, Brazil, Canada, China, Germany, Mexico, Puerto Rico, South Korea, U.K. U.S.
2	France	Carrefour	Cash and carry, convenience, discount, hypermarket, supermarket	61,565	61,565	1,069	Argentina, Belgium, Brazil, Chile, China, Colombia, Czech Republic, Dominican Republic, France, Greece, Indonesia, Italy, Japan, Madagascar, Malaysia, Mauritius, Mexico, Morocco, Oman, Poland, Portugal, Qatar, Romania, Singapore, Slovakia, Spain, South Korea, Switzerland, Taiwan, Thailand, Turkey, United Arab Emirates
3	Netherlands	Ahold	Cash and carry, convenience, discount, hypermarket, specialty, supermarket	74,723	57,976	1,207	Argentina, Brazil, Chile, Costa Rica, Czech Republic, Denmark, Ecuador, El Salvador, Estonia, Guatemala, Honduras, Indonesia, Latvia, Lithuania, Malaysia, Netherlands, Nicaragua, Norway, Paraguay, Peru, Poland, Portugal, Slovakia, Spain, Sweden, Thailand, U.S.
4	U.S.	Home Depot	DIY, specialty	53,553	53,553	3,044	Canada, Mexico, Puerto Rico, U.S.
5	U.S.	Kroger	Convenience, discount, specialty, supermarket, warehouse	50,098	50,098	1,043	U.S.
6	Germany	Metro	Cash and carry, department, DIY, hypermarket, specialty, superstore	43,877	43,357	398	Austria, Belgium, Bulgaria, China, Croatia, Czech Republic, Denmark, France, Germany, Greece, Hungary, India, Italy, Japan, Luxembourg, Morocco, Netherlands, Poland, Portugal, Romania, Russia, Slovakia, Spain, Switzerland, Turkey, U.K., Ukraine, Vietnam

(continued)

TABLE 7.1 TOP FIFTY GLOBAL RETAILERS (continued)

Deloitte & Touche Rank	Country of Origin	Name of Company	Formats	2001 Sales[a] (in millions of U.S. dollars)	2001 Retail Sales (in millions of U.S. dollars)	2001 Group Income (Loss)[a] (in millions of U.S. dollars)	Countries of Operation
7	U.S.	Target	Department, discount	39,888	39,455	1,368	U.S.
8	U.S.	Albertson's	Drug, supermarket, warehouse	37,931	37,931	501	U.S.
9	U.S.	Kmart	Discount, superstore	36,151	36,151	(2,418)	U.S.
10	U.S.	Sears	Department, mail order, specialty	41,078	35,843	735	Canada, Puerto Rico, U.S.
11	U.S.	Safeway	Supermarket	34,301	34,301	1,254	Canada, U.S.
12	U.S.	Costco	Warehouse	34,797	34,137	602	Canada, Japan, Mexico, Puerto Rico, South Korea, Taiwan, U.K., U.S.
13	U.K.	Tesco	Convenience, department, hypermarket, supermarket, superstore, specialty	33,885	33,614	1,195	Czech Republic, Hungary, Malaysia, Poland, Republic of Ireland, Thailand, South Korea, Slovakia, Taiwan, Thailand, U.K., U.S
14	U.S.	JCPenney	Department, drug, mail order	32,004	32,004	98	Brazil, Mexico, Puerto Rico, U.S.
15	Germany	Aldi Einkauf	Discount	31,310[b]	31,310[b]	n/a	Austria, Australia, Belgium, Denmark, France, Germany, Luxembourg, Netherlands, Republic of Ireland, Spain, U.K., U.S.
16	Germany	Rewe	Cash and carry, discount, DIY, drug, hypermarket, specialty, supermarket, superstore	33,260	29,078	n/a	Austria, Bulgaria, Czech Republic, France, Germany, Hungary, Italy, Poland, Romania, Slovakia, Ukraine

Deloitte & Touche Rank	Country of Origin	Name of Company	Formats	2001 Sales[a] (in millions of U.S. dollars)	2001 Retail Sales (in millions of U.S. dollars)	2001 Group Income (Loss)[a] (in millions of U.S. dollars)	Countries of Operation
17	France	Intermarche	Cash and carry, convenience, discount, DIY, food service, specialty, supermarket, superstore	28,710[b]	28,710[b]	n/a	Belgium, France, Germany, Italy, Poland, Portugal, Romania, Spain
18	Germany	Edeka/AVA	Cash and carry, discount, DIY, supermarket, hypermarket, superstore	26,700[b]	26,700[b]	n/a	Austria, Czech Republic, Denmark, France, Germany, Poland, Russia
19	U.S.	Walgreens	Drug	24,623	24,623	886	Puerto Rico, U.S.
20	U.K.	J Sainsbury	Convenience, hypermarket, supermarket, superstore	24,491	24,081	524	U.K., U.S.
21	France	Auchan	Department, DIY, hypermarket, specialty, supermarket	23,456	23,456	295	Angola, Argentina, Belgium, Brazil, China, Denmark, France, Hungary, Italy, Luxembourg, Mexico, Morocco, Netherlands, Poland, Portugal, Russia, Spain, Taiwan, U.K., U.S.
22	Germany	Tengelmann	Cash and carry, discount, DIY, drug, hypermarket, specialty, supermarket, superstore	22,980[b]	22,980[b]	n/a	Austria, Canada, China, Czech Republic, Denmark, Germany, Hungary, Italy, Latvia, Poland, Portugal, Slovakia, Slovenia, Spain, Switzerland, U.S.
23	U.S.	CVS	Drug	22,241	22,241	413	U.S.
24	U.S.	Lowe's	DIY	22,111	22,111	1,023	U.S.
25	Japan	Ito-Yokado	Department, discount, food service, hypermarket, specialty, supermarket, superstore	24,804	21,145	389	Australia, Canada, China, Japan, Malaysia, Mexico, Philippines, Spain, South Korea, Taiwan, Thailand, Turkey, U.S.

(continued)

TABLE 7.1 TOP FIFTY GLOBAL RETAILERS (continued)

Deloitte & Touche Rank	Country of Origin	Name of Company	Formats	2001 Sales[a] (in millions of U.S. dollars)	2001 Retail Sales (in millions of U.S. dollars)	2001 Group Income (Loss)[a] (in millions of U.S. dollars)	Countries of Operation
26	Japan	Aeon (Jusco)	Convenience, DIY, department, discount, drug, hypermarket, specialty, supermarket, superstore	21,960	20,040	(121)	Canada, China, Japan, Malaysia, Philippines, South Korea, Taiwan, Thailand, U.K., U.S.
27	U.S.	Auto Nation	Auto	19,989	19,989	232	U.S.
28	France	Casino	Cash and carry, convenience, department, food service, hypermarket, supermarket, warehouse	19,984	19,984	379	Argentina, Bahrain, Belgium, Brazil, Colombia, France, Lebanon, Mexico, Netherlands, Poland, Spain, Taiwan, Thailand, Tunisia, Uruguay, U.S., Venezuela
29	U.S.	Best Buy	Specialty	19,597	19,597	570	U.S.
30	Germany	Otto Versand	Mail order, specialty	19,905	19,307	64	Austria, Belgium, Canada, China, Czech Republic, Denmark, Finland, France, Germany, Hong Kong SAR, Hungary, India, Italy, Japan, Netherlands, Norway, Poland, Portugal, South Korea, Spain, Switzerland, Taiwan, U.K., U.S.
31	France	E Leclerc	Hypermarket, supermarket	19,050[b]	19,050[b]	n/a	France, Italy, Poland, Portugal, Slovenia, Spain
32	Belgium	Delhaize Le Lion	Cash and carry, convenience, drug, specialty, supermarket, warehouse	18,957	18,957	132	Belgium, Bulgaria, Czech Republic, Greece, Indonesia, Luxembourg, Romania, Singapore, Slovakia, Thailand, U.S.
33	Germany	Lidl & Schwarz	Cash and carry, discount, hypermarket, superstore	18,110[b]	18,110[b]	n/a	Austria, Belgium, Croatia, Czech Republic, Estonia, Finland, France, Germany, Greece, Hungary, Italy, Latvia, Netherlands, Norway, Portugal, Republic of Ireland, Slovakia, Spain, Sweden, U.K.

Deloitte & Touche Rank	Country of Origin	Name of Company	Formats	2001 Sales[a] (in millions of U.S. dollars)	2001 Retail Sales (in millions of U.S. dollars)	2001 Group Income (Loss)[a] (in millions of U.S. dollars)	Countries of Operation
34	U.K.	Kingfisher	Department, drug, DIY, specialty	17,196	17,196	979	Austria, Belgium, Brazil, Canada, China, Czech Republic, France, Germany, Italy, Luxembourg, Netherlands, Poland, Slovakia, Taiwan, Turkey, Singapore, U.K.
35	U.S.	Federated Department Stores	Department, mail order	15,651	15,651	(276)	U.S.
36	U.S.	Publix	Supermarket	15,370	15,370	530	U.S.
37	Japan	Daiei	Department, discount, food service, hypermarket, specialty, supermarket	18,599	15,260	(2,475)	China, Japan, U.S.
38	U.S.	Rite Aid	Drug	15,171	15,171	(828)	U.S.
39	U.S.	McDonald's	Food service	14,870	14,870	1,637	Global
40	U.S.	May Department Stores	Department, specialty	14,215	14,215	703	U.S.
41	U.S.	Gap	Specialty	13,848	13,848	(8)	Canada, France, Germany, Japan, U.K., U.S.
42	U.K.	Marks and Spencer	Department, specialty, supermarket	14,226	13,506	219	Bahrain, Belgium, China, Croatia, Cyprus, Czech Republic, Finland, France, Germany, Greece, Hungary, Indonesia, Japan, Kuwait, Lebanon, Luxembourg, Malaysia, Malta, Netherlands, Philippines, Poland, Portugal, Qatar, Republic of Ireland, Romania, Singapore, South Korea, Spain, Taiwan, Thailand, Turkey, United Arab Emirates, U.K., U.S.
43	U.K.	Safeway	Hypermarket, supermarket, superstore	13,400	13,400	354	Republic of Ireland, U.K.

(continued)

TABLE 7.1 TOP FIFTY GLOBAL RETAILERS *(continued)*

Deloitte & Touche Rank	Country of Origin	Name of Company	Formats	2001 Sales[a] (in millions of U.S. dollars)	2001 Retail Sales (in millions of U.S. dollars)	2001 Group Income (Loss)[a] (in millions of U.S. dollars)	Countries of Operation
44	Germany	KarstadtQuelle	Department, food service, mail order, specialty	14,235	12,812	208	Austria, Belgium, Czech Republic, Denmark, Finland, France, Germany, Italy, Luxembourg, Netherlands, Norway, Poland, Slovakia, Spain, Switzerland, U.K.
45	U.S.	Circuit City	Auto, specialty	12,791	12,791	219	U.S.
46	U.S.	Winn-Dixie	Supermarket	12,334	12,334	87	Bahamas, U.S.
47	Australia	Coles Myer	Department, specialty, supermarket	12,112	12,112	77	Australia, New Zealand
48	U.S.	Meijer	Superstore	11,450[b]	11,450[b]	n/a	U.S.
49	U.S.	Toys "R" Us	Specialty	11,019	11,019	67	Australia, Austria, Bahrain, Canada, Denmark, Germany, Hong Kong, France, Indonesia, Israel, Japan, Malaysia, Mauritius, Netherlands, Norway, Portugal, Qatar, Saudi Arabia, Singapore, South Africa, Spain, Sweden, Switzerland, Taiwan, Turkey, United Arab Emirates, U.K., U.S.
50	U.S.	A&P	Supermarket	10,973	10,973	72	U.S.

[a]Includes nonretail.

[b]Estimate.

Source: Deloitte & Touche, with assistance from M+M Planet Retail.

CLOSEST TO CONSUMERS

The influence of retailers comes partly from industry consolidation, but also from the relationship of retailers to their customers. One example of this relationship is the customer-loyalty plans most chains have adopted in recent years. Customers register for a card that gives them special sale prices on various goods every week. When a customer goes through the checkout counter, the store clerk swipes the consumer's card over the scanner. Then all of the purchases the customer makes on that day are scanned or keyed into the system.

The accumulation of this kind of data over a year's time can give the retailer an intimate knowledge of each customer's buying habits. The retailer can determine whether the customer has strong brand loyalty or is willing to shift brands if an item is on sale. The retailer knows what days of the week the customer shops, whether he or she uses coupons, what flavors and sizes the customer prefers, and how frequently the customer replenishes the items. The retailer knows if the customer is counting calories or fat, has high cholesterol, is a vegetarian, is a gourmet cook, or lives on frozen dinners. The retailer knows if the customer has children or pets and whether the pets include cats or dogs—and if the dog has fleas. The retailer even knows if the customer has frequent menstrual cramps. With all of the millions of dollars manufacturers invest in research, they still do not have this depth of knowledge that retailers have about their customers. And they don't meet their customers face to face once or twice a week as retailers do.

What is puzzling is that most sources say retailers have not used this personal knowledge to target customers for specific items. They also have not shared this data with manufacturers (who would love to have it). Some say that while supermarkets possess an incredible amount of data about their customers—us—they are not advanced enough technologically to take advantage of the information. Technology, however, can be bought. It is more likely that retailers do not want to be accused of invading the privacy of their customers. This could irreparably harm the delicate retailer-customer relationship. It also could attract the attention of federal regulators and organizations that promote the protection of privacy.

PRIVATE LABELS REDEFINED

Another indication of growing retailer influence has been the increase in sales of private-label goods. Private-label items, also known as store brands or house brands, account for an estimated 15 percent of total food and beverage sales, about $70 billion annually. This is expected to rise to 18 percent by 2004 (Agri-Food Trade Service website).

The whole notion of private labels has changed considerably in recent years. The so-called plain-packaged generic products that hit the market in the late 1970s and early 1980s have largely disappeared. Those were items based on the lowest possible price, introduced during an era of rapid inflation and economic contraction. Many of today's private labels, such as Safeway and President's Choice, are of a quality equal to or better than advertised brands of packaged goods from major manufacturers. They may even be more expensive, even though they are not backed by brand advertising support. Some major supermarket chains even feature two private labels, one that competes with the quality of branded goods and one perceived as a low-priced alternative but still of good quality.

Whatever form they take, house brands make the struggle for shelf space all the more intense. As the larger supermarket chains add stores and customers, they are able to buy greater quantities of private labels at lower per-unit costs. They want to carry—and must carry—national brands, but their own house brands usually yield them more profit per unit.

These brands will almost certainly grow in the future because of some demographic and psychographic trends. As consumers age, they tend to be more careful in their spending. So as Baby Boomers age, they will be more likely to look for bargains in house brands. At the same time, the younger Generations X and Y, growing into the next generation of householders, don't remember the low-quality generic goods and house brands of the past. They will have grown up with private labels and will accept them as readily as they accept nationally advertised brands.

In effect, retailers are doing what the advertising community has been doing for years: building brands. They have the basic brand equity in the retail establishment, plus the brand equity of their store brands. Perhaps Sears, Roebuck & Company—despite slipping from the top retail spot—is the best example. The retailer has built powerful brands with DieHard batteries, Craftsman tools, and Kenmore appliances. Sears, however, is not an exception, but rather part of a growing trend of retail brands that are more popular than manufacturers' brands, such as Gap jeans, Eddie Bauer parkas, and Lands' End button-down shirts.

BIGGER AND FEWER RETAILERS

Although this discussion of retail power has concentrated on the grocery area, there is plenty of evidence of growing consolidation in fewer hands in virtually every other area of retailing. An analysis of data from the *Statistical Abstract of the United States* shows declines of at least 20 percent in the number of retail establishments in several categories, including grocery stores, new- and used-car dealers, drugstores, gas stations, liquor stores, hardware stores, and shoe stores. Fewer retailers are selling larger shares of merchandise.

New-car dealerships provide an example of how influence has tilted from the manufacturer to the retailer in recent years. The number of new-car outlets in the United States has declined from more than thirty thousand in 1970 to about 21,400 in 2002 (*Automotive*

News Databook, 2002). This means the remaining dealers are selling more cars per dealership. More important, they are selling more brands of cars, setting up competitive showdowns within individual dealerships. Years ago, franchises were awarded to dealers on an exclusive basis. A Chevrolet dealer, for example, could not also be a Ford dealer. That requirement doesn't exist anymore.

The exclusivity requirement fell by the wayside as imported brands moved heavily into the market and individual dealerships gave way to group dealerships. One example of the consolidation trend is the former Mauro Auto Mall on Interstate Highway 94 in a rural area midway between Chicago and Milwaukee. The huge retail operation for years was a franchisee of nine major car brands, including such head-to-head rivals as Ford and Chevrolet, and Nissan and Toyota.

That was a classic demonstration of dealer leverage, but this example gets even more demonstrative of the power shift from manufacturers to dealers. In 1998 the Mauro operation was acquired by CarMax, one of the largest used-car dealer organizations in the country, as CarMax moved to increase its presence in the new-car business. And as another indication of retail consolidation, CarMax at the time was owned by Circuit City Stores Inc., one of the largest U.S. retailers of computers, electronics, and appliances. (Circuit City is contemplating spinning off CarMax as this is being written.)

CarMax only recently became a new-car group dealer and has grown steadily. While it has a sizable operation, it is dwarfed by Auto-Nation, Inc., which retains the distinction of being the biggest auto retailer in the United States. AutoNation operates about 285 dealerships in nineteen states, handling the Big Three U.S. car manufacturers, as well as the Big Three Japanese carmakers. In 2001 it reported sales of 454,000 new cars (plus sales of 258,000 used cars), with total revenues of $20 billion. Carmakers tread lightly when dealing with AutoNation. Just as mom-and-pop grocery stores were replaced by supermarkets, small dealerships are being replaced by automobile megadealerships.

The retail end of the auto industry is so appealing that Ford tried to move into the business in the late 1990s. Being able to make cars and sell them directly to the public would have provided Ford with plenty of marketing muscle, allowing the company to make more money and compete more aggressively with other manufacturers. Ford started buying up franchises in a few markets, but after a couple of years, decided to leave well enough alone and pulled out of the business, something other retailers were happy to see.

NOT ALL SURVIVE

While consolidation and concentration have taken place in many areas of retailing, it would be wrong to assume that all, or even most, major retailers are prospering. Fierce competition is taking its toll among retailers that lack a solid position in the marketplace. Montgomery Ward & Company, a pioneer in the mail-order business and once the operator of hundreds of department stores across the United States, went out of business in 2001. The following year, Kmart, which operated successfully for decades as the largest discounter in the country, declared bankruptcy.

Its bankruptcy was largely a matter of competition, not only from the dominating Wal-Mart and Target, but also from the growth of "category killer" operations like Home Depot, Toys "R" Us, Sports Authority, Circuit City, and others. This is not to overlook the growth of Internet E-commerce, which will be addressed in Chapter 10. E-commerce has exerted and will continue to exert a tremendous amount of pressure on the retail sector.

Consolidation in the retail area almost certainly will continue in the next few years. As few as five major supermarket chains may well dominate the U.S. grocery business within five years, and Wal-Mart will probably continue to be the biggest player. At the same time, the bulk of the grocery business will probably be dominated by no more than a dozen manufacturers. There also is certain to be continued consolidation across national borders. Much of this will take place outside the United States in regions where there are free-trade agreements, such as in Europe and Latin America. Although Royal Ahold from the Netherlands is the only retailer with a substantial presence in the United States, we can also expect other major retailers from other countries to move into the market in the years to come.

At least one other notion should be noted here. Although retailers sell products from marketing companies with national advertising budgets, they have grown into major national advertisers themselves. In *Advertising Age*'s 2002 list of 100 leading national advertisers, 20 of the leaders were retail companies, including Sears, JCPenney, Target, and Home Depot. As far as brands advertising in the United States, retailers hold an even more prominent role. As Table 7.2 indicates, fifteen of the top fifty "megabrands" in the United States are retailer brands, including fast-food restaurant chains.

As consolidation continues in the retail arena, there is little question that more retail advertisers will penetrate this list. It is just another way that retail is exerting influence on the advertising business and on marketing companies that traditionally dominated the realm of top brands. The interesting aspect of this for marketers is that retail has developed into a complex entity playing far more than its traditional role as the last link in the marketing chain.

Not only have retailers increasingly developed brand identities that might be stronger than those of manufacturers, but the retail establishment itself—whether supermarket, drugstore, or general merchant—has also become another medium. So here we have a place where consumers can be reached by marketers, not only to promote products and services, but to sell them.

TABLE 7.2 TOP FIFTY MEGABRANDS, RANKED BY TOTAL MEASURED U.S. AD SPENDING IN FIRST HALF OF 2002

RANK			U.S. AD SPENDING			SPENDING BY MEDIUM									
2002	2001	Megabrand	Parent Company	January–June 2002	Percent Change from 2001	Magazine	Sunday Magazine	Newspaper	Outdoor	Network TV	Spot TV	Syndicated TV	Cable TV Networks	Radio
1	1	AT&T telecommunications[a]	AT&T Corp./AT&T Wireless	$549,744	16.9	$14,628	$845	$213,361	$11,162	$138,693	$48,312	$8,609	$81,683	$32,451
2	2	Verizon telecommunications	Verizon Communications	515,335	34.7	12,565	311	175,817	8,694	128,422	118,703	12,877	23,808	34,138
3	3	Chevrolet vehicles	General Motors Corp.	361,773	−4.3	71,531	0	10,798	5,813	142,250	100,934	2,417	23,757	4,274
4	5	Ford vehicles	Ford Motor Co.	356,093	11.2	73,393	1,162	32,215	3,434	145,793	69,415	3,169	21,662	5,852
5	7	Toyota vehicles	Toyota Motor Corp.	327,891	14.2	97,497	1,805	20,176	3,449	94,175	79,789	29	30,785	185
6	4	McDonald's restaurants	McDonald's Corp.	285,958	−13.4	7,433	0	568	15,653	145,608	70,762	18,776	23,578	3,581
7	10	Honda vehicles	Honda Motor Co.	270,460	7.3	38,803	569	19,069	1,942	80,540	94,777	9,824	24,520	416
8	6	Sprint telecommunications	Sprint Corp.	259,429	−9.8	11,636	0	111,909	2,182	86,522	33,139	55	7,563	6,423
9	13	Cingular Wireless telecommunications[b]	SBC Communications	259,135	32.0	4,581	0	116,888	5,097	63,741	22,605	7	13,859	32,358

(continued)

TABLE 7.2 TOP FIFTY MEGABRANDS, RANKED BY TOTAL MEASURED U.S. AD SPENDING IN FIRST HALF OF 2002, *continued*

U.S. AD SPENDING — **SPENDING BY MEDIUM**

2002	2001	Megabrand	Parent Company	January–June 2002	Percent Change from 2001	Magazine	Sunday Magazine	Newspaper	Outdoor	Network TV	Spot TV	Syndicated TV	Cable TV Networks	Radio
10	16	Nissan vehicles	Nissan Motor Co.	250,278	47.5	57,467	742	10,366	1,887	86,742	75,792	3,961	11,949	1,372
11	12	Sears department stores	Sears, Roebuck & Co.	221,831	3.9	7,121	5,784	56,651	142	89,477	12,322	13,110	28,588	8,636
12	9	Dodge vehicles	Daimler-Chrysler	191,934	−27.9	27,728	0	17,504	2,448	35,807	88,199	489	11,759	8,001
13	15	Home Depot building supply stores	Home Depot	188,968	6.9	8,689	41	39,176	394	78,974	9,809	1,655	19,915	30,316
14	21	Burger King restaurants[c]	Diageo	179,206	21.3	3,792	0	1,950	2,966	75,256	13,670	35,603	26,298	19,672
15	14	Volkswagen vehicles	Volkswagen	177,393	−1.2	16,561	0	7,419	411	103,246	32,512	0	9,967	7,277
16	8	Chrysler vehicles	Daimler-Chrysler	176,344	−35.2	41,217	0	7,002	423	48,332	63,382	478	13,496	2,014
17	17	Macy's department stores	Federated Department Stores	157,346	−3.1	4,410	242	136,731	516	0	15,160	0	0	287
18	20	Wal-Mart discount stores	Wal-Mart Stores	152,790	2.6	6,937	3,608	3,644	165	59,580	40,477	7,997	29,379	1,002
19	18	Kmart discount stores	Kmart Corp.	151,861	−3.9	11,883	398	59,064	10	43,481	7,323	15,609	6,798	7,297

RANK | U.S. AD SPENDING | SPENDING BY MEDIUM

2002	2001	Megabrand	Parent Company	January–June 2002	Percent Change from 2001	Magazine	Sunday Magazine	Newspaper	Outdoor	Network TV	Spot TV	Syndicated TV	Cable TV Networks	Radio
20	27	Budweiser & Bud Light beers	Anheuser-Busch Cos.	151,044	19.3	2,802	0	1,131	5,329	112,180	14,906	353	14,333	10
21	28	Visa credit card services	Visa International	144,397	15.6	11,014	0	1,046	2,281	108,475	5,275	1,312	13,886	1,108
22	31	Wendy's restaurants	Wendy's International	140,349	17.8	18,602	0	217	3,420	67,723	16,234	16,307	16,416	1,431
23	52	Dell computers	Dell Computer Corp.	139,621	42.2	20,946	34,956	30,130	3	14,041	1,436	1,174	36,936	0
24	19	IBM computers, software, and services	IBM Corp.	139,485	−8.5	23,277	173	37,646	1,123	57,583	136	2,650	16,899	0
25	24	Target discount stores	Target Corp.	138,266	−0.4	21,251	835	46,492	972	47,885	11,993	885	6,529	1,423
26	35	JCPenney department stores	J. C. Penney Corp.	136,285	17.6	4,769	1,307	45,334	92	57,567	466	534	12,475	13,742
27	38	Nike footwear and apparel	Nike	130,330	13.9	42,497	173	446	1,966	70,138	944	454	13,164	550

(continued)

RANK 2002	2001	Megabrand	Parent Company	January–June 2002	Percent Change from 2001	Magazine	Sunday Magazine	Newspaper	Outdoor	Network TV	Spot TV	Syndicated TV	Cable TV Networks	Radio
28	36	Lowe's building supply stores	Lowe's Cos.	128,405	10.9	6,326	16	24,647	1,048	40,878	29,477	713	18,858	6,442
29	25	Mitsubishi vehicles	Mitsubishi Motors Corp.	126,803	−2.3	2,652	0	15,122	15	86,114	13,745	1,843	7,313	0
30	44	State Farm insurance	State Farm Mutual Auto Insurance Co.	124,225	20.6	25,154	7,200	9,069	4,980	52,670	2,034	3,116	10,903	9,099
31	82	Cadillac vehicles	General Motors Corp.	123,186	64.0	23,590	0	12,090	697	54,702	19,386	116	12,471	134
32	43	Kellogg's cereals and snacks	Kellogg Co.	121,911	18.3	14,022	301	175	23	41,844	8,807	24,939	29,527	2,271
33	37	Best Buy electronics stores	Best Buy Co.	120,265	5.1	9,515	0	72,711	99	17,693	14,685	0	4,735	829
34	32	L'Oreal beauty products	L'Oreal	118,341	0.3	39,559	0	738	964	52,664	383	9,088	14,944	0
35	11	Microsoft software & computer products	Microsoft Corp.	118,008	−50.8	45,760	846	8,900	1,064	40,532	7,497	0	12,786	624
36	55	Jeep vehicles	Daimler-Chrysler	117,252	21.7	18,259	0	4,574	15	29,705	55,085	355	9,018	241
37	23	American Express financial services	American Express Co.	115,382	−17.6	8,607	173	9,879	2,474	65,220	2,958	282	24,499	1,290

U.S. AD SPENDING   SPENDING BY MEDIUM

RANK | U.S. AD SPENDING — SPENDING BY MEDIUM

2002	2001	Megabrand	Parent Company	January–June 2002	Percent Change from 2001	Magazine	Sunday Magazine	Newspaper	Outdoor	Network TV	Spot TV	Syndicated TV	Cable TV Networks	Radio
38	22	Miller beers	SABMiller	114,837	−22.0	5,185	0	427	14,649	67,747	12,595	442	12,854	937
39	77	Saturn vehicles	General Motors Corp.	112,815	47.8	12,187	0	700	373	69,801	18,101	300	11,300	53
40	50	KFC restaurants	Yum Brands	110,099	10.9	0	0	203	1,044	65,865	30,122	14	12,316	535
41	51	Kia vehicles	Kia Corp. Motors	109,484	10.8	5,913	0	165	223	51,931	34,174	0	17,037	40
42	382	Nexium heartburn medicine	AstraZeneca	109,004	654.2	23,858	3,040	0	0	66,197	271	8,137	5,861	1,639
43	41	General Mills cereals	General Mills	107,444	1.4	1,808	0	60	15	36,905	41,296	26	25,718	1,617
44	48	Dillard's department stores	Dillard's	106,359	6.6	4,367	25	101,392	343	0	94	0	0	137
45	47	Mazda vehicles	Mazda Motor Corp.	106,273	6.5	258	0	22,883	13	54,569	19,567	21	8,178	785
46	49	Acura vehicles	Honda Motor Co.	104,556	5.0	31,701	1,162	7,063	9	9,285	43,161	2	12,173	0
47	86	Nextel telecommunications	Nextel Communications	102,867	38.8	2,674	0	53,604	9,143	20,851	1,252	0	7,782	7,561

(continued)

TABLE 7.2 TOP FIFTY MEGABRANDS, RANKED BY TOTAL MEASURED U.S. AD SPENDING IN FIRST HALF OF 2002, *continued*

RANK		U.S. AD SPENDING				SPENDING BY MEDIUM								
2002	2001	Megabrand	Parent Company	January–June 2002	Percent Change from 2001	Magazine	Sunday Magazine	Newspaper	Outdoor	Network TV	Spot TV	Syndicated TV	Cable TV Networks	Radio
48	79	Lexus vehicles	Toyota Motor Corp.	101,693	33.8	25,476	0	15,358	929	31,581	12,560	0	13,851	1,939
49	62	Office of National Drug Control Policy	U.S. government	99,476	17.7	13,756	3,905	9,441	2,078	51,769	6,224	887	6,574	4,842
50	66	Subway restaurants	Doctor's Associates	98,441	19.5	122	0	207	671	49,773	34,547	4,624	8,455	41

Note: Dollars are in thousands. Rankings for 2001 represent data compiled in 2002. Figures are an *Ad Age* analysis of measured media data from Taylor Nelson Sofres' Competitive Media Reporting. Newspaper includes national newspapers; radio includes network radio and national spot radio.

[a]AT&T Corporation spun off AT&T Wireless, but the two are considered one megabrand because both use the AT&T brand.

[b]BellSouth Corporation owns 40 percent.

[c]Diageo is selling Burger King Corporation to a consortium led by Texas Pacific Group.

Source: *Advertising Age*, October 14, 2002, p. S-2.

Low Price No Bargain as Brand Building Tool; Rethink Strategy if Price Is the Yardstick for Value

PETER MURANE

Establishing and sustaining market leadership through a low-price strategy is both difficult and risky. Marketers that compete solely on discounts and deals fail to understand the role pricing should play in a brand's overall value proposition. They mistake a low price for a value proposition, and risk turning their product into a commodity where the lowest price point wins.

There are a handful of successful companies that have "won" on price. On its way to increasing revenue to nearly $200 billion in 2001 from $32 billion in 1991, Wal-Mart Stores perfected the everyday-low-pricing business model. Other retailers, like Kmart, tried to match Wal-Mart's low price points only to fail at creating sustainable operating profits. Wal-Mart is one of the rare companies that built sustainable competitive advantage through a commodity-pricing strategy. But pricing alone is not the sole driver of the company's success. Wal-Mart built a distribution infrastructure so advanced and efficient that it can afford to price products for less and still generate healthy margins.

As glorious a success story as Wal-Mart is, establishing and sustaining market leadership through a pricing strategy is a very tricky act to follow. Look at the long-distance business. While long-distance usage has grown 50 percent over roughly the last ten years, the long-distance price battle that AT&T, Sprint, and MCI waged during the 1990s resulted not in a strong, brand-driven category leader but in the spotty financial performance of all major carriers. Revenue growth has been inconsistent, and churn rates remain an ongoing issue.

Unfortunately, the telecommunications industry has been slow to learn from the collapse of long-distance pricing. In wireless communications, for example, every major carrier is currently pursuing a bucket-of-minutes strategy. Prices are dropping like rocks as minutes become commodities and marketers struggle to hold onto market share. In the end, the consumer wins and the service provider is forced to sell either more minutes or more services to grow.

AN EPIDEMIC OF PROMOTIONS

Similarly, satellite dish and cable TV price promotions are an epidemic and are conditioning consumers to subscribe based on price alone. On billboards and newspaper ads across the country, competitors woo subscribers with promises of free installation, free channels, and lower monthly prices. This approach is so devoid of marketing imagination that it's no wonder the industry subscriber churn approaches 30 percent per year. Consumers have been conditioned to shop for the lowest deal versus more long-term drivers of customer retention like product offerings or service differentiation.

Marketers and CEOs must restrain themselves. It needs to be remembered that price is only one element of a brand's value proposition. By definition, the day price becomes the sole definition of value is the day that a category becomes a commodity. Unless they have a lower cost structure, most marketers that compete on price alone are simply being lazy and cannot expect to build sustainable advantage.

CREATING BRAND PREFERENCE

There is a more strategic way to meet sales objectives and drive stock appreciation, and it involves creating brand preference. Building a brand requires creativity and a longer-term horizon for measuring success. It also requires some sacrifices, like losing low-margin customers that shop only on price. But these sacrifices pay off in the long run in the form of customers willing to pay a premium for a brand's point of difference.

For example, it is well chronicled how Starbucks Coffee Company seemingly reinvented the coffee category based on the European cafe concept. What Starbucks really did, however, was rejuvenate a commodity category, improving the product and making brands matter again. The next time you purchase a $3 latte, think about how price-sensitive buying cans of coffee at the grocery store used to be.

Evian bottled water sets another brand-price gold standard. Evian is the worldwide leader in a bottled-water market that is booming. The market is not booming because of low prices (ounce for ounce, Evian is more expensive than Coke) but rather because of brands. Evian manages to lead while charging some of the highest prices in the category. And this is a category where very little noticeable product differentiation exists from one brand of bottled water to the next.

Finally, hooray for Southwest Airlines for its understanding of how pricing strategy and brand differentiation mutually support business goals. Southwest is synonymous with good value, but the brand experience is not necessarily cheap. There are lower-cost providers than Southwest, but few other airlines offer a better value. In pricing, advertising, and customer service, Southwest simply creates a better brand experience. It's no surprise that Southwest's price/earnings ratio is above the industry average.

When the price of a brand becomes its primary measure of value, categories risk becoming commodities. As a result, margins generally decline. The next time you find yourself playing the discount game with your competitors, think harder about other ways to enhance the value of your brand through product improvements, service enhancements, and good old-fashioned brand building. When price alone becomes the measure of your marketing plan, it's time to reevaluate the marketing mix.

Peter Murane (peter@brandjuice.com) is president of BrandJuice Consulting, Denver, a marketing management consulting firm specializing in building unique brands. This piece originally appeared as a "Viewpoint" article in the July 1, 2002, issue of Advertising Age.

CHAPTER 8

INTEGRATION: KEY TO THE FUTURE

Agencies Must Demonstrate that "Media-Neutral" Is More than a Pious Platitude

With the dramatic changes that have taken place in the industry over the past twenty years, the traditional advertising agencies have lost the most. When the bulk of marketing expenditures were going into television, the agencies had a clear role: do research on the mass audiences, create attractive commercials, and place those commercials on the three networks in the United States, or at least buy a selection of time on local television stations. Everything else was simply an addition to the basic television campaign. Buy some pages in national magazines, run some radio commercials in key markets, and maybe place some outdoor boards in high-traffic areas. As far as newspapers were concerned, it was up to local dealers to decide whether they wanted to use them or not.

That simple solution to advertising doesn't exist anymore. Television is not as dominant as it once was. A whole world of cable and satellite channels is now available to smart marketers. One must devote more time to media evaluation and selection, and it can produce more effective advertising. That is exactly what clients are looking for—more answers to their marketing problems. And aside from the proliferation of television, cable, and satellite signals, there has been substantial growth in all other forms of marketing—sales promotion, direct marketing, sponsorship, not to mention the Internet.

A NEW ROLE FOR AGENCIES?

The question is, What role should an advertising agency fill in this new marketing environment? An agency that doesn't reinvent itself will be relegated to the role of providing only advertising services, and there isn't much of a future if that is the only thing you produce. That role is only tactical and must be subject to a marketing strategy determined by some other entity, perhaps even a management consultant.

Appearing at an advertising conference in mid-2002, Steven J. Heyer, then president and CEO of Coca-Cola Ventures (and now president and chief operating officer of Coca-Cola Company), was asked about the future of advertising agencies and their value to clients. "Maybe in the days of David Ogilvy and before, agencies were the most valued partner a CEO could have," he asserted. "The agency business over the last twenty-five or thirty years gave a lot of that away. It gave it up to management consulting firms, to bankers—for a variety of reasons. The most serious was that [agencies] defined their contribution too narrowly, as advertising, not marketing, and as making a good creative product, not helping me build a strategy that allows me to build my position in a category.

"[Agencies] need a common vocabulary that crosses disciplines, and it hasn't been created. We want the folks in the agencies to understand our brand goals and be our strategic partners. Then we need them to be able to execute against, to use overused words, an integrated media platform. In a funny kind of way for me, it starts with a better understanding of the media plan that ties to consumer touch points more than it does to the creative idea."

Heyer's take on the role of advertising agencies is perceptive because of his broad background. He previously served as president of Young & Rubicam Advertising and also of Turner Broadcasting System. So he has witnessed the marketing function from the viewpoint of agency, media, and client.

The question was asked of Heyer because Coca-Cola had recently signed a $500 million, eleven-year deal with the National Collegiate Athletic Association and CBS-TV. Ad agencies that represent some Coca-Cola brands "are involved as advisers to the process, but the lion's share of the work was really internal to Coke," he responded.

It seems to me—and to a lot of others within the business—that agencies have to look at themselves differently. Agencies often talk about repositioning client brands. Now they have to reposition themselves to assume more strategic roles for their clients. Since clients are determined to use a variety of marketing services, the ideal role for an advertising agency would be to direct and integrate those services into a comprehensive marketing strategy for clients.

Is this happening yet? Not really, says Brian Williams, president and CEO of Element 79, a Chicago-based subsidiary of Omnicom. "Some progress has been made by agencies coordinating various marketing services, but this has been done only executionally" (personal interview with Williams, August 2, 2002). An agency, for example, has an advertising assignment from a client but is also entrusted with coordinating the efforts of a sales promotion agency or a direct marketing firm to correspond with the advertising campaign. Some agencies are doing this already.

"The notion of integration is perfectly correct," stresses Williams, "but it's not enough as it is being done now. Nobody is doing any strategic integration." That means starting right at the beginning of a project by determining the needs of a client and then planning how to meet those needs by whatever functions are necessary. Williams has a specific and relevant analogy of how this should be done: "Let's call it strategic brand architecting. The agency functions the same way an architect and general contractor would approach the building of a house. You start out with a certain amount of money from a client with the assignment of planning a campaign. You also have to start with a media-neutral strategy." This means you don't assume that most or even any of the money will go into traditional advertising—or any other specific discipline, for that matter.

The agency, acting as this marketing "architect," determines the best strategy for building the client's campaign. It then hires various subcontractors such as designers or sales promotion companies or public relations specialists to execute their segments of the strategy. The agency doesn't have to know how to execute all of these various functions, just as a contractor doesn't have to be an expert in plumbing, carpentry, and masonry. The key is that the contractor or the strategic architect must know how all of these elements should work together. It is possible that the agency might handle the advertising aspect itself (just as a carpenter-based contractor might do the carpentry on a new house), but even that is not necessary.

"What is necessary is that the strategy must be not only media-neutral, but profit-neutral," Williams adds. The architect (agency) should be able to produce a blueprint that might include no advertising element at all. Is this possible? Perhaps. But it would be difficult for an agency to create a plan that wouldn't generate a role for itself along with the compensation it would bring. That's where profit-neutrality comes in. The agency should be compensated for its planning work, aside from any advertising. Because of this, the ideal situation might be that the marketing architect is not the agency itself, but an independent affiliate of the agency, one that can evaluate and execute a plan using many forms of marketing.

A different but similar analogy regarding the role of marketing integrator comes from DDB's Keith Reinhard: "Agencies lack three things in going forward on integration. One is that there isn't enough client demand for internal integration. The CEO of a client says he wants it, but when you get down two or three layers, the demand isn't there. In fact, the clients are as siloed as agencies are. Two is that we lack the generalist discipline." Agencies should be more like Leonard Bernstein, Reinhard adds—an orchestra conductor who knows what all of the instruments and vocalists can do, writes the music, and puts the whole thing together. The third factor still lacking is a proper compensation plan for those who can choreograph such an integrated campaign.

Whether it is to be an orchestra conductor or a general contractor, the role of marketing mastermind may well have an increasingly important place in the future world of advertising.

Williams's idea of being profit-neutral and Reinhard's desire for compensation strategy is further supported by an observation made by International Advertising Association director general and former J. Walter Thompson executive Wally O'Brien: "Agencies have had difficulty implementing integrated programs because of their compensation policies. Say an account director at an advertising agency gets a certain budget to produce a campaign for a client. He or she can direct money to various types of activities like direct marketing or promotion, but if the account director is compensated based on the success only of the advertising campaign, there's no incentive to devote much money to other alternatives."

The same lack of incentive exists in the current situation where an advertising agency might be under the same corporate umbrella as a direct-marketing agency or promotion agency. If the advertising agency is overseeing the client's budget but its only compensation is coming from its advertising fees, it has little incentive to spread the wealth to its fellow corporate companies.

AGENCIES CHANGING

Many agencies will say that they are already performing integrated marketing services. There is more talk, however, than action in that regard. But even the talk is good, because it signals a change from a decade ago, when ad agencies were preaching that the only way to build a brand was by media advertising, and that some kinds of promotion could increase sales in the short run but would hurt the client's brand name in the long run.

If any integration is being done right now, it is largely coming from the clients themselves. But even then, turf wars and compensation battles are being waged at client companies. The sales manager is looking for sales promotion support while the advertising manager is trying to increase the media budget. These are classic internal client struggles.

Ad agencies are well positioned to take on the responsibility of marketing integrators as long as they respect the valuable roles other functions can serve in a multimodal campaign. This would be best accomplished if they separated the integration function from the advertising function and developed a compensation program based on their integration work alone. The danger of not doing this is that some other entity, most likely a management consultancy with marketing expertise, will move into the void.

Advertising agencies are not the only ones struggling with the problem of integration. The publishing and broadcasting companies also have been largely unsuccessful in selling multimedia packages to their clients. And just as in the agency business, it's a matter of compensation.

I have seen all kinds of plans to create "combined sales" of print and/or broadcast properties fail over the years. Here is a typical example: One publication in a group has a particular advertiser spending a lot of money, usually because that publication is its most effective vehicle. Then someone in corporate management or at an affiliated publication suggests that the company should create a "group buy," offering the advertiser a terrific deal if it would only put a few ads in the other publications. If the deal is accepted, the advertiser typically takes some money from the primary publication to get exposure in the other one. One publication gains, but the other loses.

This is not a good example of integration because the publisher with the business doesn't want to lose any of it. In fact, if the publisher did allow some business to move into another publication, it would decrease his publication's billings and perhaps even reduce his performance pay. It is the publishing company's responsibility to make sure a publisher would be rewarded for helping push business into another publication.

The same challenge is also being wrestled with by the big media conglomerates that own properties in broadcast, print, Internet, and other promotion categories. The lack of integration reportedly was one reason for the departure of Robert Pittman as CEO of AOL Time Warner Inc. in mid-2002. Pittman went to the company with a sterling background as a media innovator. He was a key player in the development of MTV in 1981, and before that was a "boy wonder" as a radio program director in Chicago. But the company apparently found it too difficult to deal on a corporate level with major clients and provide them with comprehensive programs to encompass a wide variety of media. No doubt the internal clash of corporate cultures between AOL and Time Warner managements also played a part in the change.

The history of the media business offers precious few examples in which clients were provided with tailored multimedia strategies. Ad agencies have been talking about doing this, but it might well turn out that the media-buying specialists—whether independent or owned by ad agencies—will eventually be the key players in this role, leaving even less of a strategic role for ad agencies.

INTEGRATION IS POSSIBLE

As far as the media are concerned, they might do themselves a favor by observing how some integration is taking place at the editorial/programming level. In local markets, for example, newspapers are working closely with their affiliated radio or television stations, even putting together joint Internet operations. Internationally, NBC-TV has assembled an information resource that feeds its basic network, plus CNBC and MSNBC. The same video, reporters, and anchors may appear on any of the NBC properties, whether delivered over the air, by cable, by satellite, or online. Fox is positioned to do the same thing with its broadcast network, news channel, and regional sports channels. If it works on the programming side of the business, there is evidence that it might work on the advertising side.

None of these attempts at integration, whether on the agency level or the media level, are going to succeed in the long run unless two necessary elements are present:

1. The selection of integrated services or media must be beneficial to the client and, indeed, must produce better results than any current piece-by-piece approach.
2. Whoever is doing the integrating must be rewarded for those services, in addition to any compensation earned by performing his or her regular duties.

If traditional ad agencies and the media conglomerates can't grapple effectively with client demands for coordinated and integrated programs, their inability will create a vacuum for some other entity to impose itself in the marketing process. This could create fertile ground for media-buying specialists as long as the specialists redefine media to include all forms of marketing, not only measured media.

On the other hand, some management consultants may also be well placed to take on some or all of the integration duties. If this occurred, it would be a blow to all advertising agencies. It would once again relegate them to being suppliers of advertising services and have them relating to midlevel executives at the client level while the consultants play golf with clients' top management.

Let's Fix Advertising

GRAHAM PHILLIPS

Every generation of senior ad-agency and client executives faces its own challenges. I had my share in the 1980s and '90s as chairman and CEO of Ogilvy & Mather and Y&R Advertising. But the need to innovate, instead of just reducing head count and cutting costs, and to refocus on getting results for clients seems more critical than ever before.

Advertising Age reported U.S. ad spending fell 6.5 percent last year from 2000 levels. Industry forecasters said it was the largest year-to-year decline since Great Depression year 1938, when ad spending fell 8 percent. The cause goes beyond the current recession and the death of dot-coms. It reflects fundamental weakness in the advertising process. This can be fixed with a more disciplined creative product, new agency/client work structures that emphasize greater speed and efficiency, compensation schemes that focus agencies on producing great ideas that generate results for clients, and a resolution to the problem of commercial saturation on TV.

FIX THE CREATIVE PRODUCT

Too much of today's advertising is irrelevant and a waste of money. Ten years ago, some observers opined that ad agencies seemed "more interested in selling their product than the client's product." Since then, it's gone from bad to worse. Next time you watch a TV commercial, ask these simple questions: Does it contain an idea? Is the idea relevant to the selling message? (Nine times out of ten, it isn't.) Does the idea have legs? (Is it campaign-able? Can it be run for years?) Does the commercial reward the viewer for watching? Does it impart useful information? Make me feel better about the brand? Few meet these criteria.

The industry needs to refocus on getting results for clients via better training and discipline. Creative people should be rewarded based on results they generate for clients, not awards they win. Put together a portfolio of ads that are creative and have generated results, and use this as a template and training tool. Agencies that produce great ads that get results are the most profitable, win more new business, and attract the best people. Why wouldn't the industry focus more on creating work that gets results?

FIX THE CREATIVE PROCESS

Most clients have completely changed how they do business to improve productivity, product quality, customer service, and so forth. Agencies have done little to change the way they create advertising. The process is inefficient, unproductive, and not conducive to greater speed and lower costs.

Currently, a team of agency people and the client develop strategy. After a great deal of time and money has been spent, the task is handed to a few creative people. They often work on other clients' business as well, and this can create a bottleneck situation. Usually, the rest of the team and the client are excluded from the development of creative work. As a result, first creative efforts are often wide of the mark—causing more delays. Why not keep the entire team and the client involved in the idea-generating phase?

Who says ordinary mortals cannot come up with a great ad idea? Wouldn't it be sensible to involve the client in the entire process so that selling the end result would be a foregone conclusion?

A word on planners: Their job is to distill huge amounts of information into a simple insight that can drive a powerful creative idea. But I've often been presented with incomprehensible hundred-page documents. Keeping it simple would make planners and the creative process more productive.

FIX AGENCY COMPENSATION

Many clients have told me they feel their agencies are paid too much for too little. That perception, in combination with a mediocre creative product, explains why clients have become less loyal to their agencies. I am a proponent of fee-based incentive bonus systems that reward the agency handsomely for a big idea that gets results. Perhaps this reward should work more like a royalty payment over the life of the idea rather than a one-time bonus payment. A big idea has enormous value. Shouldn't that value be paid for over the life of the idea? Clients should not begrudge the agency making significant profits in return for significant results. There should be no compensation limits on the upside in return for lower going-in costs.

FIX TV-COMMERCIAL SATURATION

There are nearly 40 percent more commercials and promos on network TV today than ten years ago: sixteen minutes per hour. Cable TV can contain more than eighteen minutes per hour. Are we not killing the goose that lays the golden egg? Let's see more effort to merge program content and advertising into a seamless format. It will require the cooperation of broadcasters, writers, producers, and ad people, but something must be done to reduce TV ad clutter.

■ ■ ■ ■

Lack of confidence in advertising as an effective marketing tool may be contributing to the current downturn. Refocusing on getting results for clients and becoming more innovative is essential advice for the industry to heed.

Graham Phillips (GrahamP@aol.com) is a former chairman and CEO of Ogilvy & Mather and Y&R Advertising. He is a director of Brunswick Corporation and consults for a number of other companies. This piece originally appeared as a "Viewpoint" article in the May 20, 2002, issue of Advertising Age.

REINVENTING MEDIA, AND OTHER VARIATIONS ON THE THEME

Old Media Are Leading the Development of New Media—with Some Tech Twists

The annual meeting of the American Association of Advertising Agencies in 1994 returned to the Greenbrier after having been held at other locations for several years. It was to be a momentous meeting. The prime speaker was Edwin L. Artzt, then chairman and CEO of Procter & Gamble. There is no greater draw for an advertising agency audience than to hear a person who heads the largest advertiser company in the country. Artzt was even better than his billing. He delivered a speech that was to be discussed in the advertising community for years afterward.

The audience listened intently as Artzt warned that agencies and advertising itself had to change if they were going to survive what he saw as the possible future of the business. Here are some excerpts from his remarks:

> Our most important advertising medium—television—is about to change big time, and we have one whale of a stake in these changes. From where we stand today we can't be sure that ad-supported TV programming will have a future in the world being created—a world of video-on-demand, pay-per-view, and subscription television.
>
> Within the next few years—surely before the end of the decade—consumers will be choosing among hundreds of shows and pay-per-view movies. They'll have dozens of home-shopping channels. They'll play hours of interactive video games. And for many of these—maybe most—no advertising at all. . . .

Frequency and depth of sale in advertising are critical to preserving loyalty to frequently purchased brands like ours. For example, in any given month, P&G brands like Tide and Crest and Pantene will reach more than 90 percent of their target audience six or seven times.

The only way you can achieve that kind of impact is with broad-reach television, which is why we spend almost 90 percent of our $3 billion advertising budget on TV, and why we simply must preserve our ability to use television as our principal advertising medium. . . . The most important change, by far, is that people will become more program-driven and less channel-driven. What that means is we may lose access to broad segments of our audiences because program-driven viewers will no longer stay tuned to a particular channel. In fact, they may not even stay tuned to ad-supported programming at all.

The shift toward program-driven viewing isn't new. It began when the first alternatives to the networks appeared—the early independents. And then as the UHF dial filled up and cable came on the scene, people got used to switching among more and more channels to find what they wanted to watch. But the trend accelerated in the eighties as a result of a simple new technology—the remote control, the zapper. And remote controls were just the beginning. They'll soon be replaced by program navigational services that will fundamentally change the dynamics of TV viewing. . . .

Here is another chilling thought. There is a very real possibility that the majority of programs people watch will not be advertising-supported. . . . Now we've got competition, not just among traditional, ad-supported media, but from unadvertised programming as well—entertainment and information that will represent an

entirely separate source of revenue for media suppliers and
programmers alike.

This is a real threat. These new media suppliers will
give consumers what they want and potentially at a price
they're willing to pay. If user fees replace advertising
revenue, we're in serious trouble.

Artzt's speech stirred the agency organization to join with
the Association of National Advertisers to form the Coalition for
Advertising-Supported Information and Entertainment. The mission
of the organization is to research new media alternatives and reach,
but also to have advertisers get into the creation and production of
programming.

Little, however, has been accomplished by the coalition except
the research aspect. Broadcast television continues to lose its share
of audience to other media. HBO, once a mere purveyor of second-
run movies, has challenged broadcast television with such series as
"The Sopranos," "Sex and the City," "Oz," and "Six Feet Under." The
shows have received a substantial amount of critical acclaim and are
also drawing larger audiences. When a new "Sopranos" series aired
in September 2002, it attracted more viewers than any of the network programs in that time slot.

As a subscription service, HBO does not carry advertising. Nevertheless, the cable channel has 26 million subscribers. These are
people who might otherwise be watching broadcast television. Given
the sometimes rough and adult content of these programs, they could
never run on broadcast television, probably not even on basic cable.
Even if the networks could carry such "nonfamily" programming,
there is no question that P&G and most other national advertisers
would not put their commercials on them.

In fact, so much of broadcast television has become violent, sex-
ually oriented, and vulgar that many advertisers are withholding their
messages from these programs. Forty major advertisers have formed

a coalition, the Family Friendly Programming Forum, and have put development money into several series they feel are appropriate for the whole family to watch (*Electronic Media*, June 10, 2002).

This might bring some advertising dollars to television, but it probably will not attract that many additional eyeballs. The industry is facing a situation where it is more difficult to capture and hold the attention of the audience. Because of this, new media ideas are tumbling out of the woodwork.

Although "new media" in the late 1990s usually referred to some kind of Internet application, much of the so-called new media is coming from old-media companies with a boost from technology. The next chapter is devoted to the Internet and other digital forms of communication. This chapter looks at new media options for advertisers, some of which combine two or more technologies.

COMMERCIAL-FREE COMMERCIAL TELEVISION?

One example of merging technologies is the interactive television technology being rolled out by Wink Communications Inc., which was acquired by a subsidiary of Liberty Media Corporation in 2002. The company licenses its technology to twenty-six programmers, including the major broadcast and cable networks, and is available only through satellite or digital cable.

Viewers who want television interactivity get free subscriptions to the service, which includes a set-top box and remote-control device. If an advertiser has made a deal with Wink, when its commercial appears on television, a Wink icon appears on the screen, and viewers can click on it for interactivity. The advertiser may offer free samples, do research, offer coupons, and so forth to get the viewers involved.

But that is only one way to use the service. If, for example, a vocalist appears on a television variety or talk show, his or her record company could have the opportunity of selling the artist's CD directly to viewers who like the music. That takes us only one step away from something that would be a radical step ahead: the marriage of product placement and interactivity.

We have all seen movies in which the protagonist drinks a certain brand of beer or drives a particular make of car. Are these simply tactics by the director to make films more realistic by using real products? I asked that question to a Hollywood acquaintance a few years back, and he laughed. "Nothing gets into any scene of a motion picture by accident," he said. "Everything is there for a purpose. Either the company paid for the placement, or it made a deal to reciprocate by promoting the movie in its own advertising."

While product placement is well established in movies, it has not made major inroads into television. CBS, however, has sought out and attracted a handful of marketers who placed their products on some of that network's so-called reality programs, including "Survivor" and "The Amazing Race" (*Advertising Age*, September 23, 2002).

With the Wink technology and that of other interactive companies, television producers will be able to make deals with advertisers and write specific products and brands into their programs. The characters on "Friends," for example, could easily meet in a Starbucks coffee shop rather than the imaginary Central Perk Café they frequent. That kind of plug could be far more powerful than just another television commercial.

Is there a greater significance to this? For one thing, it might develop a whole new generation of television programming without commercial interruptions. It would probably be unethical to have "stealth" advertisers. All of the product placements should be announced in the opening credits and probably again at the end of the programs. But this form of commercial-free commercial television is not unrealistic. It also is not exactly what Edwin Artzt was considering when he discussed commercial-free television at the 4As meeting. He may, in fact, like this form of noncommercial advertising.

Viewers might actually be more willing to tune into a program like this because of the lack of interruptions. It is certain they would at least watch in the beginning because of the novelty factor. I'm not sure anyone ever tuned into any other regularly scheduled television program to watch the advertising.

This form of marketing gives advertisers some concrete benefits. Advertisers could save the cost of producing commercials, as long as they were somehow able to deliver an effective message simply by product placement. More than that, they would still have the added feature of interactivity, allowing them to run contests, collect data from viewers, and so on.

The notion of advertisers being involved in the development of programming is not new. In the early days of radio, sponsors "owned" the programming. Many years ago, I worked with a gentleman named John Hayes Kelly, who was an advertising account executive in the 1930s. John handled the Studebaker account, and he often recounted that he hired the talent for the car company's radio program, approved the scripts, and in effect acted as the producer of the show. (John also said he went on the road with Studebaker executives, making presentations to dealers around the country and giving advice to salespeople. That's when advertising was an extension of sales, not an entity unto itself.)

Television in its early days also had sponsored programs, such as the Hallmark "Hall of Fame," in which the advertiser and its agency were closely involved with the programming. Only when the cost of television time escalated did advertisers move away from sponsorship. Broadcasters bought programs from production companies and started selling spots to several advertisers on a single program. This is a major reason for the current state of advertising clutter on television, along with the trend to thirty- and fifteen-second commercials and station promos and away from sixty-second commercials.

A NEW ENEMY: PERSONAL VIDEO RECORDERS

The personal video recorder (PVR) is not a new medium as much as it is a new way for viewers to consume an old medium. This change is exactly what Edwin Artzt was concerned about in that 1994 speech.

Using PVRs, such as TiVo and ReplayTV, television viewers can program their units to record their favorite programs and watch them at times that are more convenient to them. The old video recorders allowed users to record only one or two hours of programs. The PVRs can accommodate up to sixty hours of programming. These are actually computers with hard drives on which the programming is stored, a technological leap from the recording tape of VCRs. More than that, PVRs can be programmed to record a consumer's favorite show every time it plays. They can also be programmed to record any show that features a consumer's favorite actor, athletic team, hobby, or other area of interest.

Since the programs are recorded, viewers then are able to zap through the commercials. The advantage is that a viewer would be able to see a professional football game in sixty minutes, rather than the three-plus hours it usually takes with all of the commercial breaks, time-outs, and other interruptions.

Technology is also available for viewers to program their units to eliminate all commercials, harking back to Edwin Artzt's fears. But it has also attracted the attention of everybody in the advertising chain. Perhaps the most outspoken critic of PVR technology was Jamie Kellner, chairman of Turner Broadcasting System, who was quoted in *Cable World* magazine as saying that viewers who zap commercials are "stealing" the programming (*Cable World*, April 29, 2002). Kellner later said his comment was misinterpreted and was quoted as explaining, "Before we damage the economics of this industry, which are fairly frail on the network side . . . before the American people go off and think that this whole thing can go on without them watching commercials, we should all understand what the cost is going to be" (*Denver Post*, July 16, 2002).

His concern is understandable. If a substantial number of viewers are going to block out commercials, advertisers will pressure television and cable networks to adjust their pricing downward.

If there is a positive spin for broadcasters, it is that PVR sales are moving slowly; PVRs are estimated to be in about only 1 percent of U.S. households. Nevertheless, these figures will most likely increase in the future, depending heavily on whether pricing of the units and of the monthly subscription fees declines. Another factor is the technological traffic jam being caused around the family television set. An early-adopter family might already have a cable or satellite set-top box, an old VCR, a laser disc player, and a DVD-CD unit, not to mention the stereo player and maybe a cable modem with a wireless keyboard.

Not only the cost of the hardware but also the monthly subscription fees will slow the growth of the next new technology, whatever it turns out to be. A technology-friendly family that scrutinizes its monthly spending on cable TV fees, Internet service provider subscriptions, cell phone charges, pager rates, pay-per-view fees, and all the rest might be shocked at the total.

One thing that cable and satellite have shown the marketplace is that it is possible to have programming without commercials. A certain percentage of the public will pay a reasonable subscription fee for programming without commercials. As the quality of programming on subscription television improves—and if the trend toward cheaper programming on broadcast television continues—that percentage is likely to increase. What is developing is the stratification of market segments into those that can and those that can't afford to pay for their programming. The question remaining for broadcast is, How much are advertisers willing to pay for an audience that excludes the most affluent consumers?

Not to confuse readers with the numerous new technologies, but I should mention the development of video-on-demand (VOD). This is yet another set-top box option that would allow cable viewers to order up anything from a motion picture to a sporting event to a news program. There is no definitive plan on the pricing of this service, although it probably will be offered on some kind of subscription basis. Promotion was just beginning in late 2002, and it will take months, if not years, to determine whether this will have a significant place among the panoply of media options.

PUBLISHERS GO DIGITAL

It didn't take traditional media long to recognize the potential that the Internet offered to enhance their basic product. Within only a few years after the World Wide Web became operable in 1994, thousands of radio and television stations, magazines and newspapers, cable networks and publishing companies were setting up their own websites.

They weren't going to make the same mistake consumer magazines did fifty years earlier, when they tried to compete with television rather than learn how to use it for their own benefit. They also realized that they had a couple of valuable assets they could bring to a new medium. They owned content, which would be difficult for any newcomer to develop, and they owned national or international brands.

Going digital was a no-brainer for magazines and newspapers (although many struggled against the idea in the early days of the World Wide Web). The publications were known entities. They had bases of loyal readers, good reputations, and a body of expertise in their field of interest. They also had subscription lists, contacts with advertisers, and a considerable amount of knowledge about their readers that they could apply to an Internet product.

By 2000 an evolutionary change had become evident. Although the websites were created to bolster the reach and image of the core media, they were starting to take on a life of their own. Salon.com and Slate.com were started as digital "magazines" right from the start. They were not Internet versions of existing publications.

Gradually though, traditional media realized that their Web entities had developed their own audiences and their own personalities. Companies created business plans, hired separate staffs, made major investments, and set off to create a new concept that is generally called online publishing. This concept achieved a more concrete status in mid-2001, when the Online Publishers Association (OPA) was formed. Its core members include some of the best-known brand names in media: the *New York Times*, CBS, ESPN, the *Wall Street Journal*, *USA Today*, *Forbes*, and even France's *Le Monde*.

The list of respected members lent credibility to the association, but even more so to the reality that this was the genesis of a legitimate new medium. It is, however, still a young and undeveloped player in search of its place in the marketing landscape. As far as business plans are concerned, it appears that most online publishers are seeking to establish revenue formulas similar to those of their parent entities, according to Michael Zimbalist, executive director of the OPA:

> Most media, with the exception of broadcast television, rely on a combination of advertising and circulation revenues for the business models. The ratio of advertising revenue to subscription revenue is about three to one, or 75 percent advertising to 25 percent subscription. Online publishing hasn't reached that point yet as far as payment for online content is concerned. Only about 9 percent of online publishing revenues come from paid content, but that amount is increasing and we expect that it will eventually be pretty close to the traditional media ratio (personal interview with Zimbalist, August 14, 2002).

According to OPA research conducted by comScore Networks, the total market for online content in 2001 was $675 million. (This does not include sex-oriented and gambling sites.) Through the first part of 2002, the amount increased by 155 percent over the preceding year, perhaps indicating that this will grow into a sizable market. The area that seems to hold the most potential for growth of online revenues is that of business content, which represents nearly 32 percent of all online content revenues. Entertainment and lifestyle content is next in line, with nearly 17 percent.

Table 9.1 shows the 25 websites with the highest paid content revenue. Actual dollar amounts are not reported.

In terms of revenue generation, the top website is real.com, which has a broad consumer audience and offers a wide range of games, music, and other entertainment features. The champion among paid-subscription sites is the *Wall Street Journal's* wsj.com, which had more than 650,000 paid subscribers as of mid-2002. The OPA estimates that 1,700 sites charge for online content, but 97 percent of the money spent for content goes to the top 100 sites.

Ever since online publishing started in the late 1990s, one of the most commonly repeated themes was, "Everybody is on the Internet, but nobody is making any money from it." That statement will probably be disproved in short order. Those who have valuable information and develop valuable audiences will be able to make money on both the subscription and the advertising sides of the business. In the magazine business, it can take as long as five or ten years for a publication to become profitable. It may well be that the same rule will apply to Internet publications.

MULTIMEDIA PUBLICATIONS

The development of digital technologies may also provide publishers with a new way to reach readers. One of these technologies is accomplished through the use of portable document format (PDF) files.

TABLE 9.1	TOP TWENTY-FIVE WEBSITES, RANKED BY PAID CONTENT REVENUE

Rank	Domain	Content Category
1	real.com	Entertainment/lifestyles; games
2	wsj.com	Business content
3	match.com	Personals/dating
4	yahoo.com	Personals/dating; business content; sports; research; entertainment/lifestyles
5	consumerreports.org	Research
6	ancestry.com	Community directories
7	weightwatchers.com	Personal growth
8	1800ussearch.com	Research
9	matchmaker.com	Personals/dating
10	consumerinfo.com	Credit help
11	lee.org	Business content
12	classmates.com	Community directories
13	playboy.com	Entertainment/lifestyles
14	thestreet.com	Business content
15	msn.com	Games
16	kiss.com	Personals/dating
17	espn.go.com	Sports
18	carfax.com	Research
19	hallmark.com	Greeting cards
20	bluemountain.com	Greeting cards
21	arttoday.com	Business content
22	britannica.com	Research
23	elibrary.com	Research
24	changewave.com	Business content
25	smartmoney.com	Business content

* 1,700 sites are estimated to be charging for content online.
* 85 percent of money spent for online content goes to 50 sites.
* 97 percent of money spent for online content goes to 100 sites.

Source: Based on comScore/OPA research. Copyright (c) 2002 Online Publishers Association (OPA).

Without getting too technical (because I wouldn't understand it), virtually all magazines and newspapers are typeset and formatted electronically. These electronic files are often sent directly to printers, which transform them into printing plates and eventually produce the publications we read on paper.

These same electronic files, however, can also be E-mailed to a subscriber or posted to a website. And they can be read using the basic Adobe Acrobat software, which is offered free to users. Readers can turn the pages, just as they would read a magazine. They can also enlarge or condense a page, see one page at a time, or view facing pages. Perhaps of most importance to publishers is that readers can see all of the advertising in the publication.

Sounds great, but there are some obstacles to overcome. Perhaps the most frequently spoken question in publishing in the last five years is, "But who wants to read a magazine on a computer?" Of course, reading on a computer isn't all that handy, although it has become less cumbersome now that notebook computers are lighter and screens are sharper.

In response to this question, I would say that we have become accustomed to reading a lot of things on computers, not the least of which are billions of E-mail messages every day. Many of us have become accustomed to doing research on the Internet, perhaps not reading for pleasure, but certainly for information, for news, for advice. In fact, we are already reading on computers.

Let's add some other features to this PDF version of a magazine. Imagine you could have a search function, so that when you receive the publication, you can type in your company name or your competitor's name and see whether it is mentioned in the publication. That can be pretty handy if you want to find something right away. Also imagine that because of the magic of the digital world, you could incorporate audio into the file. If there is an article about an interview with a person, you can click on an icon and hear a few seconds of the person speaking. It would give the reader a better measure of the person.

Also imagine that you could embed video in the magazine. This could be a strong editorial tool, in which you might demonstrate how a product is made. More than that, the technology could be used by an advertiser. A reader might click on a full-page ad and see the advertiser's television commercial running on his computer. It doesn't have to be a commercial as such. It might be a PowerPoint presentation giving the reader a more detailed look at a product being advertised. Along with this, of course, every ad offers a hyperlink to the advertiser's website. A toolbar at the bottom of the page could invite readers to buy a product, request a salesperson to call, ask for information to be mailed or E-mailed, or enter a sweepstakes.

Every bylined article could have a hyperlink to the reporter who wrote it. There's also a hyperlink to the editor and one to the circulation director in case the reader is having problems with the subscription or wants to send a gift subscription to someone else.

The great thing about all of this fantasy is that it isn't fantasy. It is real; it already exists and has an excellent chance of growing in the years to come. Even without the interactivity just described, the advantages of electronic publishing are many and benefit everyone:

- The *reader* gets immediate delivery of the publication without waiting for the paper carrier or the U.S. Postal Service. The delivery can be at home and at the office and anywhere else the reader wants it and has a computer at his or her disposal. The reader can also archive the publication if desired and if there is enough memory to handle the digital files.
- The *publisher* can eliminate three major elements of overhead, the notorious "three Ps" of paper, printing, and postage. Subscriptions are sold, renewed, and distributed via the Internet. The issue sent electronically is exactly the same as the print version, so there is no extra production cost. But the biggest advantage to publishers is that the same advertisements appear in the PDF version as in the print

version. Publishers don't have to worry that an electronic version without advertising would cannibalize print subscriptions. More than that, publishers could charge more for the advertising because of the interactive advantages of the PDF version.

- The *advertiser* benefits because it can implement a multimodal communications campaign. It can describe and explain a product more efficiently. And with interactivity, a reader can easily place an order, ask for more information, or invite a salesperson to call. All of this can be done without requiring the reader to pick up a telephone or put a letter into the mail.
- Even *society* benefits because electronic publications don't have to cut down trees or use various chemicals necessary for the printing process. More than that, electronic publishing doesn't create any waste paper that must be incinerated or transferred into garbage dumps. Environmental organizations would embrace this form of publishing.

So why isn't everyone publishing electronically? There are several reasons. One is that most advertisers haven't created advertising campaigns for this new medium. As we pointed out earlier, the challenge of integration has still not been mastered. It will take more time and more experience.

There is also something of a problem with reader acceptance in that one must have a respectable amount of computer memory and sufficient access speed in order to download these files in a reasonable amount of time. Digital publishing works much better on broadband than it does with conventional telephone lines. Technology is moving ahead, which might solve this problem.

If I sound like a cheerleader for this technology, it is probably because I was involved early on when *Ad Age Global* (then *Advertising Age International*) was invited to serve as a beta test for a new interactive PDF technology back in 2000. The company producing the interactive versions, Qiosk.com (now qMags.com), asked us to be a guinea pig for the technology as well as the business plan.

We had a specific problem with our publication for which PDF delivery was an excellent solution. Since half or more of *Ad Age Global*'s circulation was outside the United States, delivery to distant locations was very inconsistent. Subscribers in some countries might have to wait ten to fourteen days to receive their hard copies. Being able to have them receive it on the day of publication was a remarkable improvement. Being able to avoid the ever-increasing postal charges was equally important.

Since then, the advertising recession of 2001 and 2002 has caused our company to suspend the print version of *Ad Age Global*, but the publication still lives in a digital format. Other companies have since entered the digital publishing field, notably Zinio Systems Inc. and Newsstand, Inc.

As of late 2002, about two dozen magazines and newspapers, including the *New York Times* and the *Boston Globe*, were offering PDF subscriptions, identical to their print versions. This doesn't mean that this particular technology will be here forever, or even for the next couple of years. Technology is changing too rapidly to make that kind of prediction.

This we know: PDF subscription fulfillment is already a reality, but the interactivity that is available has so far not attracted much attention from advertisers. It might well be that the pressure to employ this technology will eventually have to come from clients who realize the marketing power it can produce. Its time may not yet have arrived.

INTERACTIVE TELEVISION

For years, seers have been predicting that interactive television—the combination of cable television and the Internet—will be the wave of the future. Although this marriage of media has made only minor inroads to this point, there are indications that it may grow much more rapidly in the future. This is not strictly a new medium, but it is a combination of two established media that can alter how we consume media.

It hasn't been technology that has held up the expansion of interactive television, but rather the difficulty in putting together the right deal between Internet service providers and the cable operators. In late 2002, a complex deal was in the works between AOL Time Warner and Comcast Corporation that may push the idea ahead rapidly. Comcast at the time was in the process of acquiring AT&T's cable operations.

The object of the deal is to give AOL the right to offer Internet access to a portion of Comcast subscribers via the cable company's broadband connection. That would then create a media showdown of epic proportions, featuring AOL's Internet service versus Microsoft Corporation's MSN service, the nation's second largest Internet service provider.

At least two aspects of broadband Internet access are important to users. The basic one is that it gives Internet users far faster response time over a cable connection, as opposed to a conventional telephone line or even DSL. An Internet service provider offering significantly faster response time would have an advantage in selling subscriptions over providers that did not have the same broadband speed. This part of the marriage of cable with computer is already moving ahead rapidly as cable companies launch campaigns to switch customers from telephone lines to broadband. But it is only the first step in blending cable with the Internet.

The next step would be to allow users to be watching cable TV while they are on the Internet. Even this concept isn't all that new. An entrepreneurial company called WebTV Networks Inc. introduced a technology with that capability in 1996. It gave cable viewers access to the Internet through a remote-control device or a wireless keyboard. A year later, Microsoft acquired the company and blended it into its MSN TV operation. (The Wink Communications application previously mentioned also is a variation on this form of interactive television.)

The simultaneous cable-computer connection offers consumers, programmers, and advertisers real-time, two-way communications. The programming implications could be dramatic. Interactivity could be a part of the programming as well as the advertising. Users might watch the televised drama of a criminal court trial, then vote for acquittal or conviction as if they were members of the jury. No one, including the producers, would know until the final moments what the outcome of the trial would be.

Viewers might also act as television critics, giving thumbs up or thumbs down to pilots of proposed series. (That would probably drive programming executives crazy.) Given the importance political analysts have put on voter polls in recent years, this method of assessing public response could also affect decisions made and positions taken by government leaders.

As with other forms of interactivity, advertisers would also be able to mine the viewing audience for their opinions on new products, determine the effectiveness of commercials, or use the technology to gather sales leads or actually sell products to viewers. Much of the planning for this interactivity, however, seems to fall back on a couple of old functions—the ability to chat on the Internet while a program is running or the opportunity for viewers to participate in games, or even virtual casino gambling, subject to legal restraints.

GOING TOO FAR?

As telecommunications moves into another phase of its rapidly changing life, there has been increasing discussion about the notion of beaming advertising to consumers' cellular telephones and personal digital assistants. This idea supposedly is to become more likely as technological advances improve the quality of the small screens on these devices.

You can count me as a skeptic of this proposed new medium. If consumers hate telemarketing calls at home and at work, they will definitely despise getting unwanted calls on their cell phones. Who wants to be interrupted by an advertising message while having lunch with a client or when driving the kids to school?

The ideas floated around include those of a restaurant being able to make automated calls during late morning, inviting the person to stop in for lunch or even offering a special price for that day. Another idea includes technology that will allow a retailer to send a message automatically to anyone walking by the store, offering a discount on merchandise.

As with any advertising medium, there tends to be a curiosity factor that might attract a response to any kind of new communications device. But any executive who starts getting five or six advertising calls a day on his cell phone, pager, or PDA is going to change service providers or turn the device off.

AN ENDLESS STREAM OF NEW MEDIA

Not all new media are based on advances in technology. Some forms of what we call new media are simply new places for advertisers to put their marketing messages. Or they can be new places for old media. There are many examples of that, including sponsored video newsfeeds in skyscraper elevators, video commercials on small screens mounted on gasoline pumps, and advertising in public school venues such as gymnasiums, buses, and hallways. You get a message while traveling to work or class.

Panel advertising on taxicabs is nothing new. Traditional London taxis have been wrapped with advertising for years. But in 2000, a company was offering drivers in Los Angeles $350 a month if they would have their private cars wrapped in advertisements for products (*American Demographics*, October 2000). In 2002 a company called Airport Media Inc. was attracting major advertisers who wanted their advertising wrapped on parking shuttles continually circulating through airports. The advertisers were trying to target frequent travelers.

An Orlando, Florida, company called Entry Media Inc. has been promoting a medium called Turnstile AdSleeves. These sleeves fit over the arms of turnstiles at sports stadiums and have attracted advertisers such as Coca-Cola, Compaq Computer, and Verizon Wireless. Sleeve advertising has been sold at many locations, including New York's Yankee Stadium and Wrigley Field in Chicago (Entrymedia.com).

During the short time it was fashionable for professional basketball players to shave designs and messages in their hair, British Knights Inc., maker of athletic shoes, decided this could be a new medium. The company paid bicycle messengers in New York $50 to sculpt the brand's logo in their hair.

About the same time, Fila USA and the shoe retailer Foot Locker joined together to put up 625 basketball backboards on New York City playgrounds. The boards carried a message urging students to stay in school, but they also carried the logos of the two advertisers.

In Vienna, more than 1,500 bicycles have been put on the city's streets in 2002 for anyone to use for free. The only catch is that the bikes carry the names of advertisers, with telephone companies Nokia and T-Mobile among the first clients. The costs to the advertisers: $43 per month per bike for the first month, descending to $29 for subsequent months (*Daily World Wire*, August 31, 2002).

Sony Erickson Mobile Communications Ltd. wanted to get some attention for its mobile phones that can also take pictures. The company did this by hiring sixty actors and actresses to play roles in a "guerilla marketing" scheme. The actors frequented tourist spots, bars, and other venues. They might ask passersby who might be good prospects to take their picture with the telephone/camera. Or they might have the telephone ring while the actor was in the midst of a group of people at a bar. The actor would answer the call and pop up the picture of the caller on the telephone's screen. This was a way to generate buzz for the product, and it came at a price: $5 million for a sixty-day campaign (*Wall Street Journal*, July 31, 2002).

In Denmark, a media marketing agency called Nymedie is offering new parents free baby carriages decorated with advertising messages. Parents can choose from the styles of "Push Prams" offered at the company's website and use them free of charge for two and a half years. Initial advertisers have included a bank, a fashion retailer, and the maker of Lego toys (*Daily World Wire*, August 10, 2002).

As you can see, there is no shortage of ideas of how to reach consumers in an environment of saturation advertising and proliferating media. Nothing appears to be off limits as a medium for advertising. Is this good for advertising? I don't think so.

ANOTHER VOICE . . .

Entertaining New Ideas

RANDALL ROTHENBERG

The argument once was that advertising can entertain but it must also sell. Now it seems advertising is not just entertaining but melding into the entertainment landscape itself as marketers flock toward product placements and arty ad "films" and pay to have their brands written into the plots of TV shows. This is more than simply a new twist on the old "brought to you by" sponsorships that were common when

TV and radio were in their infancy. It's a seismic shift that's here to stay. And it's largely a positive one, provided marketers remember one key tenet: a brand message must not overwhelm or dictate content.

The Madison & Vine phenomenon figured into no fewer than three *Ad Age* stories last week alone. Hal Riney, the man who helped redefine advertising with his signature style of TV commercial, declared the thirty-second spot dead. The nation's number two advertiser, Procter & Gamble Company, arranged for product placements as part of its $350 million cross-media pact with Viacom Plus. And TiVo, the ad-skipping service that has all of Madison Avenue nervously looking over its shoulder, is experimenting with extended-form ads and promotions, betting viewers will choose to view ad content if it's as compelling as the programming.

Getting people to watch ads is one thing. Making sure they still are distinguishable as ads is another. Viewers are savvy enough to know why "Survivor" contestants won Pontiac Azteks rather than Range Rovers. Writing Revlon into "All My Children" or Federal Express into "Cast Away" lends verisimilitude to the plot; but ploys, such as having Barbara Walters burble over Campbell's soup on "The View," can backfire on both the advertiser and the program pitching the product.

News shows, in particular, should not be a forum for product placement; doing so degrades the credibility of the program and will eventually turn off viewers, who will then turn off the channel. After all, that's entertainment.

Journalist and author Randall Rothenberg is director of intellectual capital for Booz Allen Hamilton management consultancy. This piece first appeared as an article in the June 24, 2002, issue of Advertising Age.

THE INTERNET AS CHANGE AGENT

Reinventing the Way We Communicate, Buy, Sell, Invest, Date, Send Greeting Cards, and Book a Trip

I t is not an exaggeration to state that the Internet is the most revolutionary new medium to be developed since television in the late 1940s and '50s. So far, it has not been as effective an advertising medium as television, but its multidimensional adaptability supersedes that of any other medium.

Writing a book about the Internet's effect on advertising is difficult. One reason is that Internet and computer technology in general is changing so rapidly and constantly. If a writer, at any one point in time, says, "This is where we are," by the time that book is published, we would already have moved through a series of new frontiers. Further complicating the situation is a continuing lag between what is possible technologically and what most business enterprises or consumers are willing to invest in. The compressed advances of technology have made it difficult for the management of many companies to attempt to stay current. For example, as I related in the previous chapter, publishers already have the technology to deliver subscriptions in PDF format, including full editorial and advertising interactivity, as well as audio and video capability. It is only the diffidence of advertisers and consumers that has delayed the widespread implementation of this technology.

It reminds me of a conference I attended a few years back, in the fledgling days of the Internet. The conference was aimed at explaining how a company might create a home page and develop a presence on the Internet. One panel included three or four speakers who had already taken the big step for their companies. A participant explained how she and her ad hoc Internet team members had little support from their management. They had to scrounge equipment from different sources and do a lot of work on their own time because the company wasn't convinced of the potential of the Internet as a business tool. Despite this, the woman was included in the panel because her group succeeded in its mission. After weeks of work, the group had established the first home page for its employer, IBM.

Since this is a book about the future, this chapter will attempt to show not only what the Internet has done but what it has the capability of doing. I will limit myself to the current state of the art, although any discussion of the future will have to assume the growth of broadband availability and the continuing increase in computer chip memory.

TECHNOLOGY'S MARKETING FLAW

I feel obliged at this juncture to mention a dicey disconnect between technology and marketing. There is a huge gulf between developing a new and marvelous technology and finding a market for that technology. This phenomenon has been evident for many years. I can trace it at least back to my youth and the introduction of the ballpoint pen. (Yes, I am that ancient.) Until then, we had only pen and ink. So when the early revolutionary versions of the ballpoint pen were introduced after World War II, one company promoted its product as being able to write underwater. The early pens cost ten times as much as fountain pens, so it was necessary to stress the differences. There did not exist, however, any body of research that could identify a substantial number of people who were itching to write underwater. This was long before scuba equipment was developed.

The funny thing is, although ballpoints actually could write underwater, what the early versions couldn't do very well was write in the pressurized cabin of an airplane. That deficiency was eventually noted and overcome by the manufacturer, and ballpoint pens have developed into one of the most ubiquitous products in the universe.

This is not an isolated incidence of technology's lack of marketing purposes. A few years back, some technology people were trying to convince audiophiles that they should upgrade their stereo systems. They were supposed to invest in a new technology called quadraphonic sound by buying new electronic equipment and deploying at least four speakers in their living rooms instead of two. The market evidently wasn't ready for that, and sufficient sales never materialized for quadraphonic sound to be the new audio standard in the American living room. The technology didn't disappear, though, and the principles of quadraphonic sound can be found today in the Surround Sound systems employed in movie theaters and advanced home "entertainment centers."

Here's another example. In 2000, a company called Digital-Convergence introduced a device called the CueCat. This was a small scanner shaped like a cat (as opposed to a mouse) that was to be connected to a computer. Several publications, including *Forbes* magazine, cooperated with the company by embedding mini bar codes in their magazine's editorial material. Anyone reading the magazine could scan the bar code and get connected directly to a relevant website.

DigitalConvergence and its partnering publications reportedly distributed 10 million CueCats free of charge in a mass mailing to users (including me). The device attracted all kinds of publicity but met with very little market enthusiasm. It appeared that most people didn't want to be online while reading a magazine. A few questions about privacy also contributed to the lack of response. The grand experiment ended within a year, aided by the fallout in the technology business.

DigitalConvergence still maintains a website, although it has only one page, and it advises visitors to hang on to their CueCats because the technology will come back again. I will save mine as a testament to developing products for nonexistent needs. And it might be a valuable collector's item for my great-grandchildren.

On an even larger scale, the early days of the then so-called home computer were fraught with marketing lapses. Any number of companies with chip technology decided that the consumer market was where the future growth was. They were going to make computers especially for the home market. The problem was, there was little need for computers in the households of that day.

Manufacturers were touting the use of computers in the kitchen, where they could facilitate such heavy-duty computing chores as storing menus and cataloging Christmas card lists. Oh, yes, and the kids could play electronic games on them.

As with any such device, interest in the hardware did not take off until a sufficient selection of software was available to accomplish many tasks. But the most powerful reason for the breakthrough success of the home computer was the development of the modem and the availability of the Internet and, ultimately, the World Wide Web. They provided plenty of motivation for the public to start communicating online and exploring the Internet.

Fifty years earlier, we could have applied the same principle to television. In those days, television stations programmed only a few hours a day, and the product was often little more than radio with pictures. It was four or five years until consumers started buying television sets in great numbers, when the quantity and quality of programming available made it worthwhile for them.

IS THE INTERNET AN ADVERTISING MEDIUM?

In one manner of speaking, it is a bit of a misnomer to call the Internet a medium, as in an advertising medium. Despite all of its many capabilities, the Internet has yet to prove itself as an effective advertising medium. This is not as much an inherent failing of the Internet as it is of marketers who have not yet mastered an advertising technique. They may someday, but it will take a lot of time and creative energy.

The Internet, though, has made its greatest impact on society as a personal communications medium and a business-to-business sales medium. It is how sons and daughters at college communicate with their parents at home. It is how corporate lawyers transfer drafts of contracts to each other. It is primarily how business operates across the world and across time zones.

It is also, to the consternation of many, the way a legion of flimflam operators engage in the not-so-nice practice of wholesale spamming. They are trying to sell us everything from Bibles to pornography to diet plans to wrinkle removers. In a twinkling, it seems, we have gone from a flood of junk mail to a tsunami of junk E-mail.

Some of the spam is downright criminal. For several years, many executives and others in the United States, including me, were receiving fraudulent letters from con men in Nigeria. Their pitches were all similar. They claimed to be officials in the previous government who were going to leave the country with $50 million. If you gave them your bank account number, they would transfer the money into your account, then at a later date, they would remove the money, leaving 10 percent behind for your cooperation. These scam letters apparently have stopped coming via the postal service but are now flowing in through E-mail. Instead of receiving a letter every three or four months, I am getting similar E-mail messages every three or four *weeks*.

Unless there are radical changes, the spamming—and the scamming—will continue, if for only one reason: it doesn't cost the sender anything. The higher postage rates rise, the more economical it is for marketers to move from "snail mail" to E-mail. There are no definitive reports on the topic, but we can assume that the response rate to spam is extremely low, and most likely getting lower, as computer users develop an immunity to these pitches. That, of course, is bad news for legitimate marketers or anyone else trying to communicate with clients and friends or do legitimate business on the Internet.

As I stated earlier in this chapter, the multidimensional adaptability of the Internet is what makes it superior to all other media. In fact, one of the Internet's strengths is its capability of distributing many other media. One example is Internet radio. Through various services, you can listen to your favorite radio station via the Internet's "streaming media" capability. There is an ongoing dispute over royalty payments, and the federal government has gotten involved in the process, but the important factor is that it is technologically possible.

And if radio is possible, why not television? With faster bandwidth, a traveling executive should be able to tune into her hometown nightly newscast via a laptop computer, viewing the local headlines and weather forecasts. This is not all that unusual, since executives are already reading the online versions of their local newspapers while they are out of town.

Television on your laptop may not be all that far in the future. As this book was being written, Northwestern University in Evanston, Illinois, announced that it was offering twenty channels of cable television to its students through the school's high-speed data network. Virtually every student has a computer and network access, and the offering allows them to watch cable without buying a television set or establishing an individual subscription. The service is offered to students for $120 per year, a bargain compared with the normal charge of $45 or more per month for a cable subscription (*Chicago Sun-Times*, September 23, 2002). Once again, this isn't a new medium, but the marriage of two existing media in one convenient package.

A MULTIFUNCTIONAL MEDIUM

Although the Internet has not developed into a proven advertising medium, its ability to deliver other media is remarkably valuable. And delivering media content is only one function of the Internet. If you add that function to the sea change in personal communications caused by E-mail, it adds up to an influential package with incredibly more potential.

There is even more the Internet can do. E-commerce has only recently begun to have an impact on the retail segment of the market. The potential for increased consumer commerce on the Internet is boundless.

In this context, it is significant that consumer E-commerce constitutes only a fraction of the business-to-business commerce already taking place. According to an estimate by eMarketer, Inc., an Internet research company, worldwide B-to-B E-commerce reached nearly $825 billion in 2002. The company also predicted that Internet B-to-B commerce would hit $2.4 trillion by 2004. Much of this business is in industrial products, such as chemicals and raw materials, and involves servicing programs in which customers can replenish supplies simply by reordering via the Internet. This streamlines the marketing process for B-to-B companies and speeds up the fulfillment process.

The marketing of office products provides an example of that. A salesperson calls on potential customers and determines what kind of products each customer routinely uses. Salespeople even estimate the amount of printer cartridges, stationery, pencils, and other items the company uses and at what rate they should be replenished. After the salesperson has established the core of products, the customer's office manager can simply go online to reorder supplies. The marketer can also determine approximately when clients should need refills and send a message prompting them to place an order.

The same kind of system can work for consumer E-commerce, although consumers don't buy at the same high dollar levels as commercial clients. Nevertheless, consumer spending on the Internet has reached respectable levels in only a short period of time, and the potential for growth is unlimited. Table 10.1 shows ten major categories of products and services being sold via the Internet, plus the year-to-year growth for the first half of 2002. Keep in mind that this growth was recorded even as the economy was flirting with a recession. Online sales in total increased 44 percent in what was otherwise a punk period for retail sales.

Another way to gauge the growing presence of the Internet is by examining its traffic in actual numbers. Research from comScore Media Metrix for July 2002 showed that properties owned by AOL Time Warner attracted the most unique (unduplicated) visitors, nearly 100 million (see Table 10.2). In real numbers, this means about 35 percent of the nation's residents visited these sites during the month of July. MSN-Microsoft sites, meanwhile, attracted nearly 90 million visitors. These are huge numbers, comparable with television's reach. More than that, we must consider that computer users are *interacting* with websites, as opposed to the passive nature of tele-

TABLE 10.1	FASTEST-GROWING CATEGORIES OF CONSUMER ONLINE SPENDING, FIRST HALF 2002 VERSUS FIRST HALF 2001

CONSUMER ONLINE SPENDING

Rank	Category	Sales, 1st Half 2002	Percent Change from 2001
1	Furniture and appliances	$ 316,189,127	154%
2	Home and garden	899,882,381	101%
3	General services	201,415,914	80%
4	Sports and fitness	482,503,210	77%
5	Travel	14,773,387,316	71%
6	Event tickets	1,249,576,972	68%
7	Office	3,218,368,617	51%
8	Video games	121,492,909	47%
9	Computer hardware	4,662,862,978	45%
10	Movies and video	434,872,979	39%
	Total Online Sales	**$34,588,658,423**	**44%**

Source: comScore Media Metrix, a division of comScore Networks Inc.

vision viewing. They are more involved with the Internet than they might be with a medium that has no interactive capability. These figures are based on comScore Networks' continuously monitored panel of 1.5 million computer users separated into target audiences at home, work, university, and outside the United States.

An interesting pattern is that more E-commerce is taking place while consumers are at work than at home. Fully half of the consumer E-commerce in fiscal 2001 (estimated at $53 billion) was conducted from at-work computers. This excludes auction sites and purchases by large corporations. E-commerce from homes in the United States was 31 percent of the total, 15 percent was from non-U.S. sources, and 4 percent from schools. The non-U.S. purchases are an interesting figure because they show the capability and the potential of international sales, far more than other media can produce.

One of the factors the research can identify is the hour of the day users are on the Internet and making purchases. The hour-by-hour research shows that E-commerce is very light in the early-morning hours but jumps considerably between 8:00 and 9:00 A.M., rising to a peak between 11 A.M. and noon.

This information can help marketers in their coordinated campaigns, according to Daniel Hess, vice president of comScore Networks Inc. "It would be myopic to overlook the many ways in which comScore's information can improve the efficiency of offline marketing efforts," he says. "For example, if online cash registers start ringing in a given product category at 8:00 to 9:00 A.M., a marketer would be wise to test share-boosting campaigns on morning TV and drive-time radio." In other words, traditional media can be used to drive E-commerce if the advertising people learn more about how and when potential customers are online and ready to buy. It's another demonstration of the use of integrated marketing.

The notion of computer use at work was also brought out in a study conducted by Millward Brown Intelliquest for the Online Publishers Association in early 2002. For those who use the Internet at

TABLE 10.2	**TOP FIFTY INTERNET PROPERTIES, AUGUST 2002**		
ALL DIGITAL MEDIA	**UNIQUE VISITORS**		
	Home/Work (123,461,000)	Home (117,920,000)	Work (42,469,000)
AOL Time Warner Network— Proprietary and WWW	97,152,000	86,583,000	29,906,000
MSN-Microsoft Sites	90,430,000	78,642,000	33,132,000
Yahoo! Sites	83,969,000	70,845,000	27,588,000
Google Sites	37,354,000	29,364,000	14,466,000
eBay	34,408,000	26,000,000	11,698,000
Terra Lycos	33,977,000	26,763,000	11,081,000
About/Primedia	31,646,000	23,870,000	10,596,000
Amazon Sites	27,347,000	19,766,000	10,041,000
Viacom Online	21,627,000	16,191,000	6,322,000
Classmates.com Sites	21,462,000	16,836,000	7,080,000
CNET Networks	20,412,000	14,505,000	7,385,000
Walt Disney Internet Group (WDIG)	20,396,000	16,808,000	6,403,000
iVillage.com: The Women's Network	19,947,000	14,057,000	5,923,000
InfoSpace Network	19,730,000	14,767,000	6,666,000
AT&T Properties	17,821,000	14,748,000	7,179,000
Real.com Network	17,726,000	13,375,000	6,486,000
Excite Network	16,401,000	12,957,000	6,310,000
eUniverse Network	16,050,000	12,881,000	4,014,000
Ticketmaster Sites	15,897,000	11,285,000	6,392,000
Gannett Sites	15,198,000	9,760,000	6,658,000
Vivendi-Universal Sites	15,119,000	11,405,000	4,509,000
AWS Technology	15,030,000	11,841,000	3,934,000
Verizon Communications Corporation	15,025,000	9,497,000	5,767,000
Gator Network	14,096,000	11,526,000	4,019,000
Ask Jeeves	13,535,000	9,532,000	4,715,000
Monster.com Property	13,401,000	9,556,000	4,829,000
Expedia Travel	13,114,000	8,260,000	5,928,000

	Home/Work (123,461,000)	Home (117,920,000)	Work (42,469,000)
SBC Communications	12,969,000	9,371,000	4,384,000
The Weather Channel	12,794,000	9,622,000	5,876,000
EA Online	12,278,000	10,016,000	2,661,000
Earthlink	11,598,000	8,875,000	3,930,000
United Online, Inc.	11,460,000	10,411,000	2,492,000
American Greetings Property	11,356,000	8,588,000	3,365,000
New York Times Digital	11,298,000	7,395,000	5,143,000
Orbitz.com	10,889,000	7,720,000	4,860,000
Sony Online	10,817,000	7,527,000	3,859,000
X.com Sites	10,360,000	7,274,000	3,903,000
CoolSavings.com	10,329,000	7,020,000	3,470,000
Columbia House Sites	10,288,000	7,348,000	4,430,000
BeMusic Sites	9,909,000	6,971,000	4,014,000
Dell.com	9,745,000	6,006,000	4,160,000
Citigroup	9,265,000	6,495,000	3,660,000
Travelocity	8,979,000	5,837,000	3,967,000
WalMart.com	8,929,000	6,858,000	2,924,000
Harris Interactive	8,914,000	6,089,000	3,433,000
UPS.com	8,825,000	5,029,000	4,281,000
Trip Network Inc.	8,388,000	5,514,000	3,112,000
News Corp. Online	8,276,000	5,948,000	2,783,000
MyFamily Network	8,195,000	5,534,000	2,673,000
Atomshockwave Sites	8,180,000	5,841,000	2,770,000

Audience: Home/work in the United States; persons aged 2+. Figures refer to number of unique visitors during the month of August 2002.

Source: comScore Media Metrix, a division of comScore Networks Inc.

work, it is their primary medium, taking up 34 percent of their "media minutes," compared with 30 percent for television. Among those who connect with the Internet at home, television consumes 44 percent of their media minutes, compared with 26 percent for the Internet.

What advertisers also must factor into these numbers is that those who use the Internet at work are more likely to be in that valuable age cohort of eighteen to thirty-four and tend to be better educated and more affluent. In marketing parlance, this means Internet users are a more valued target market (Online Publishers Association/MBIQ Media Consumption Study, November 2001). Many retailers are finding a substantial market in the Internet. Table 10.3 is a sample; it lists the top twenty-five online retailers for a particular month.

The growing power of E-commerce can also be demonstrated by the experience of traditional catalog merchants such as J. Crew. The company set a record in February 2002, when its online sales surpassed its catalog sales for the first time in history. A company executive was quoted as saying that the average online transaction was bigger than the average catalog sale, "mostly because we're able to do things online that we can't do with the catalog" (*New York Times*, March 25, 2002). What the retailer could do included programming the sales software to offer a complementary accessory as soon as a customer places an order for a particular item. A customer who buys a pair of jeans can immediately be offered an appropriate belt or top to go with the jeans.

The Internet's potential to sell goods and services is bound to increase in the years to come because of several factors, ranging from the growing penetration of Internet households to the greater willingness of consumers to use credit cards in their online purchases.

While Amazon.com has proved itself to be the E-commerce champ in terms of visitors and individual sales, companies like Dell demonstrate another factor: it is possible to sell big-ticket items on the Internet, especially if the seller has a strong brand name.

Another category that is expected to see increasing sales over the next few years is online purchasing of airline tickets. The percentage of U.S. airline tickets sold online is expected to grow from 10 percent of all sales in 2000 to 31 percent in 2005 (International

TABLE 10.3   TOP TWENTY-FIVE ONLINE RETAILERS, MAY 2002

Website	Average Purchase	Dollar Share of Market	Worldwide Visitors (in millions)
Dell.com	$1,329	22%	12.5
Ticketmaster.com	159	12	7.8
Amazon.com	45	10	49.8
OfficeDepot.com	150	10	3.5
Quill.com	159	4	0.4
Quixtar.com	126	4	0.7
Staples.com	159	3	2.1
Sears.com	282	3	4.3
QVC.com	68	3	1.9
OfficeMax.com	204	3	1.3
VictoriasSecret.com	102	2	2.8
SonyStyle.com	907	2	2.5
JCPenney.com	102	2	3.0
1-800-Flowers.com	61	2	2.9
TigerDirect.com	399	2	1.4
Newport-News.com	87	2	1.4
HSN.com	90	2	1.7
BarnesandNoble.com	71	2	9.0
ColumbiaHouse.com	43	2	11.7
Tickets.com	111	2	1.3
Proflowers.com	45	1	2.2
FTD.com	67	1	2.0
Spiegel.com	177	1	2.0
Overstock.com	97	1	3.1
Chadwicks.com	91	1	0.9

Source: comScore Networks Inc.

Data Corporation/eMarketer, April 2001). The research company eMarketer has used baseline figures from the U.S. Department of Commerce to project that online retail sales will grow from $27.3 billion in 2000 to more than $109 billion in 2005. For the same period, online travel revenues are expected to increase from $13.4 billion to more than $46 billion (eMarketer, September 2002).

Another so-called product category that has migrated effectively to the Internet is the trading of securities. In 1999, 7.2 percent of all U.S. households did some trading online, and this share is expected to grow to more than 31 percent by 2005 (Jupiter Research 2001, derived by eMarketer, April 2002). Figure 10.1 graphs this trend.

FIGURE 10.1   PERCENTAGE OF U.S. HOUSEHOLDS TRADING ONLINE, 1999–2005

Percent of Total Households

Note: Data for 2000 based on Census Bureau count of 105,480,101 total U.S. households; data for other years based on U.S. Census Bureau projected household growth rates from May 1996.

Source: Jupiter Research, 2001; derived and copyright © by eMarketer, Inc., April 2002.

BRANDING'S INTERNET VALUE

The growth in online marketing will tend to increase the importance of branding. It is not likely that many consumers would spend hundreds of dollars or more on an Internet purchase unless they were familiar with a brand name and had confidence in the quality of the product and its maker.

Mass merchandising had a tremendous impact on the importance of brand equity because of the self-service nature of retailing. Consumers relied on brand names because there were few or no salespeople to help them evaluate products. E-commerce makes brand names even more important because of the long-distance nature of the sales decision. It would be fruitless for any product with little or no brand value to compete with a highly regarded brand item.

It also stands to reason that the function of gathering research online before making a purchase will become more important in this Internet Age, as has happened with prospective car buyers. Even though they may eventually place their order with a salesperson at a car dealership, millions of Internet users do extensive research online before making that first visit to the dealer.

Predicting Marketing's Future at the Dawn of the Age of E-Commerce

BRUCE MASON

Making predictions is easy. Just ask the people who fill our lives with forecasts about what will or won't happen on January 1, 2000.

In my business—the business of advertising—technology already has set our world spinning. Advances in digital technology move faster than a speeding microchip. In fact, it's the most rapidly changing, most quickly adopted technology in the history of mankind. By the time I finish this piece and E-mail it to *Advertising Age*, the future may have taken another dramatic turn.

This we know for certain: Digital technology has opened the floodgate to electronic commerce. And electronic commerce has changed buying behavior faster than anyone believed it could. Starting with the business-to-business sector—with its installed computer base—and moving swiftly through millions of homes in the United States, Europe, and elsewhere in the world, E-commerce has taken hold.

Online sales are exploding. The Web and electronic commerce already have begun to spawn whole new global businesses—e.g., Amazon.com, E*Trade, eBay.

What we see is nothing less than the dawning of a global "digiconomy"—a new form of global distribution and sales that bypasses bricks and mortar and the traditional infra-structure usually associated with the marketing of goods and services. For whole hosts of industries, E-commerce is a faster, cheaper, and far more effective way of selling goods and services anywhere in the world.

TRANSACTIONAL TV

I predict the next pivotal event—and in my humble opinion it will occur within the next two years—is the transformation of the passive TV into an interactive transactional tool. Consumers won't need computers to surf the Web in pursuit of buying products and services. They'll be able to connect with the Web right on their TV set.

What makes this transformation possible is broadband technology.

Rupert Murdoch already has started rolling out this technology to his BSkyB satellite subscribers across Europe and, with his recent deal with Echo Star, the United States won't be far behind. John Malone and Tele-Communications Inc. are hot on his trail with the same capability in cable.

The magic of broadband technology is that, unlike narrowband, constrained by phone wires and modems, it brings high-resolution, full-motion, interactive video to the screen. Images on the Web, for the first time, will be TV quality.

The disadvantages of narrowband electronic commerce as we now know it—blurry images, disconnected or jumpy movements, flat graphics, and slow response time—will be a thing of the past.

Once again the emphasis will be on content; and creativity will never be more important.

Here's how it will work. The consumer sits at home, enjoying a TV program, and sees a commercial. If the advertising is compelling and the viewer is interested in the product, he or she can simply click the remote. The commercial will be seamlessly hot-linked to the advertiser's website, where the consumer will experience the brand real time and, if he or she desires, be able to buy the product or service right then—at the moment of brand truth—right off the TV set.

THE MOST POTENT MARKETING WEAPON

With the dawning of transactional TV, brand values will draw as much from the real-time Web interaction as from the traditional TV commercial. Transactional TV will be the most potent global marketing weapon marketers have ever seen. The business model for our clients and for us will be significantly and permanently altered.

In addition, it opens a new era of accountability. For, as John Wanamaker said at the turn of the last century, "I know half the money I spend in advertising is wasted. The only problem is that I don't know which half."

At the turn of the new century, in the new digiconomy, we'll know which half is wasted—and so will our clients—because every visit to a website and every transaction are a data point that can be tracked. That's accountability.

ROLE OF ADVERTISING AGENCIES

Along with the accountability comes a new universe of possibilities. And the role of advertising agencies—those that take a leadership role in managing real-time data and in harnessing the creative potential of transactional TV—will be more important than ever.

For those of us in the advertising business—and, actually, for those of us in all businesses—this will be the most exciting time any of us has experienced. So tighten your virtual seat belts. We are on warp speed once again.

Bruce Mason retired as CEO of True North Communications in 1999. This piece originally appeared as a "Viewpoint" article in the March 29, 1999, issue of Advertising Age *.*

CHAPTER 11

WHO ARE THESE PEOPLE ANYWAY?

They Are Older, Richer, Hipper, and More Media Savvy
than Any Other Generation of Consumers

One of the great challenges facing marketers and their ad agencies in recent years has been that of exploring and understanding the different demographics of succeeding generations. In virtually every country that has a vibrant middle class, the most economically active group—usually those aged eighteen to thirty-four—are substantially different from their parents in many ways.

Generations are dynamic—constantly changing. Just because your mother used Bab-O, the foaming cleanser, that doesn't mean you will. In fact, that might specifically be the reason you don't use the product. This was best exemplified by the "This isn't your father's Oldsmobile" campaign, though it failed to boost sales of that make. (The generation gap had nothing to do with the Olds failure. General Motors muddied up its brands by putting most of them on the same platforms, then dressing them up in models that all looked pretty much alike. What in the world do car buyers perceive as the differences among an Oldsmobile, a Pontiac, and a Chevrolet? Answer: Not much. Olds was the most vulnerable brand.) It is interesting to note that while Oldsmobile was trying to exploit some kind of antisenior attitude to attract young buyers, Buick was actively creating special promotions aimed at older drivers.

To get an overview of how the U.S. population changed over the last seventy years of the twentieth century, let's look at Table 11.1, which shows data prepared by the U.S. Census Bureau. As you can see, some of the changes are remarkable. While 1930 may seem like ancient history to younger people, thousands of Americans who were born in or before 1930 are still alive. They realize these changes have taken place within their life span.

TABLE 11.1	HOW THE NATION HAS CHANGED SINCE THE 1930 CENSUS	
Demographic Measure	**1930**	**2000**
Total U.S. population	122.8 million	281.4 million
Leading country of birth of foreign born	Italy (1.8 million)	Mexico (7.8 million)
Life expectancy	59.7 years	77.1 years
Median age	26.5 years	35.3 years
Population of California	5.7 million	33.9 million
Number of people aged 65 and over	6.6 million	35.0 million
Proportion of women in the labor force	24 percent	61 percent
Percentage of households consisting of people living alone	8 percent	26 percent
Average number of people per household	4.1	2.6

Source: U.S. Census Bureau factsheet published March 28, 2002.

Those born in 1930 and before, in the matter of a life span, have seen tremendous economic, social, political, and technological change. They were born into a world without television, fax machines, computers, mobile telephones, jetliners, microwave ovens, portable radios, Social Security, photocopy machines, stereo sound systems, penicillin, and any number of other products that today's consumers don't give a second thought to.

More than that, during their lifetime, advertising has developed into a constant, sometimes annoying, element in their lives. Advertising has affected our buying habits, altered our language, changed our fashions, and always strived to attract our attention. It also has woven its way into the culture not only of Americans but of consumers in virtually every country of the world.

At the core of modern advertising is market research, the study of consumers and what they want and how they want it. The most expert marketing people use this research to create and sell products they know will appeal to consumers. There are times, though, when research is compromised by prejudice and habits. As sophisticated as the industry is, it sometimes misses the obvious.

I published a book in 1990 called *FutureScope: Success Strategies for the 1990s and Beyond*. The object was to show that it was not all that difficult to look into current data and make some fairly accurate predictions about the future. Among the predictions in that book was that the unemployment rate would decline about the middle of the 1990s. Along with this, the book suggested that the crime rate would also decline throughout the 1990s. This was not a wild guess that just happened to pan out favorably. It was based on age statistics, the most basic demographic factor.

The number of eighteen- to thirty-four-year-olds in the United States had grown from about 39 million in 1960 to more than 70 million in 1990, an increase of about 80 percent. But that age cohort was expected to decline to about 62 million between 1990 and 2000. That meant some 8 million fewer workers would be entering the labor market. If one were to assume even moderate economic growth during the decade, it was a certainty that unemployment would decline.

Furthermore, since people in that age cohort commit most of the crime in the world, it was also easy to predict that the crime rate was also going to drop, as it has in most American cities. There was yet another nuance regarding the crime rate attributed to that decline in the age group. If the unemployment rate declines, more people are working, and there are jobs for those who might otherwise resort to crime if they were unemployed.

Let's apply this same concept to a real marketing challenge of the 1990s, which happened to be a very difficult decade for most big U.S. beer companies. Microbreweries were being hatched by the hundreds in big cities and college towns. There also was an increasing taste among beer drinkers for imported products, from countries as diverse as the Netherlands, Mexico, and China. One other factor also was at play: that same decline in the number of eighteen- to thirty-four-year-olds. People in this age group are the most conspicuous consumers of beer. If the average person in that age segment consumed only one case of beer a year, the decline in that age cohort would mean a decline of eight million cases sold. In fact, total beer sales did decline by 4 percent between 1990 and 1995 (Beer Institute). Sales have since started moving ahead again as the number of eighteen- to thirty-four-year-olds has started upward again.

When markets decline, the most common knee-jerk reaction by clients is to find a new advertising agency. They react as if they expect a new agency will be able to somehow create a few million more consumers of their product. In fact, the agencies all responded to the decline in their core audience by producing yet more commercials aimed at that shrinking market of young adults. We have all seen the typical commercials of model-handsome young hunks and shapely women in clingy dresses, some looking barely old enough to drink, socializing at singles bars. Brewers tried every juvenile advertising tactic, from Spuds McKenzie to the Swedish Bikini Team, but beer sales continued to slide. Market share may have changed, but the bigger problem of a shifting demographic wasn't even addressed. And it could have been addressed by the brewers' advertising.

I am not aware of a single beer campaign launched in the 1990s that, for example, was aimed at the thirty-five- to fifty-year-old market, a slightly older cohort that was growing by 29 percent during that decade. That group comprises the youngest members of the Baby Boom generation. Is there a reason they stop drinking beer when they hit thirty-five? Can it be because the product is no longer being advertised to them, and they are looking for something more age-appropriate? Or is it because they saw their favorite brews suddenly fragmented into a dizzying array of ice beers, red beers, dry beers, bottled draft beers, and other oxymoronic alternatives?

I am not an insider in the brewing industry, not privy to any particular research on this topic, but as a casual observer of human nature and consumer buying habits, I wonder why no brewer even tried to explore this slightly older market. Why not create a beer for the slightly more mature drinker? Why were all of their energies devoted to launching a generation of novelty beers (most of which bombed) that were sure to be avoided by the mature drinker?

More than that, the brewers should have been preparing years in advance for the decline. They should have known about the decline in their key market segment at least ten years earlier because there was the same proportionate drop in the eight- to twenty-four-year age group during the 1980s. All the brewers had to do was conduct some simple research, read the figures, and project them into the future.

But don't cry for the brewers. Beer sales are on the rise again. I maintain that it is because the number of eighteen- to thirty-four-year-olds has already started to grow and will continue to increase substantially in this decade. But I still wonder why none of the brewers is aiming a product at the fastest-growing segment of the population, Baby Boomers moving into their senior years.

And to expand one more idea on that notion, it would be interesting to see a brewer develop a beer specifically aimed at woman drinkers, the way Philip Morris Company has done with its Virginia Slims in the cigarette business. Just because your mother didn't drink beer, it doesn't guarantee that your daughter won't. Brewers already know that women generally prefer light beers; they might develop a product with a more feminine image.

Let's take a look at some of the changes taking place among some key demographic groups.

THE MATURE MARKET

Table 11.2, which lists Census Bureau population projections by age groups between 2001 and 2010, shows the trends behind an important measure: the median age of American residents. The median age hit 35.3 years in the 2000 census, meaning that half of the country's residents were older and half were younger than 35.3. That is the oldest median age ever recorded since the United States started the census. By comparison, the median age in 1980 was 30. Back in 1800, it was about 16, although not nearly as scientifically recorded as it is now.

This same aging of the population, by the way, is happening in many parts of the world. It is most evident in Europe, where aging of the population is being looked at as a potential societal problem. Populations in Western Europe have median ages that are a couple of years older than in the United States, but the birthrates are plummeting, particularly in Germany, Spain, and Italy. These countries, along with virtually all of Europe, are facing declining populations and, as a result, older populations. By 2020, the median age in Europe is projected to be 45, compared with 37 in the United States. In Italy, it is projected to be 50. Italians, once known for large families, now have one of the lowest birthrates in the world (Peter Francese, *Wall Street Journal*, March 23, 1998).

Along with lower birthrates, higher life expectancy produces an older population. In the United States, the life expectancy for persons born in 2002 was slightly more than seventy-seven years, the oldest in history.

The marketing implications of this aging are easy to discern. There will simply be a growing market for products and services con-

TABLE 11.2	PROJECTED AGE DISTRIBUTION FOR UNITED STATES		
	POPULATION		
Age Group	July 1, 2001	July 1, 2010	Percent Change
0–19 years	78,780,000	81,113,000	2.96%
20–34	56,075,000	60,002,000	7.0%
35–49	65,150,000	61,670,000	−5.4%
50–64	42,733,000	57,363,000	34.2%
65 and over	35,063,000	39,715,000	13.27%

Source: U.S. Census Bureau, January 2000.

sumed by older people. These goods and services include not only nursing homes and pharmaceuticals, but also Caribbean cruises and golf course homes.

For the marketing person, the challenge is to find out the needs and wants of the mature consumer. Meeting the challenge will necessitate a mind shift for advertising in general, which has always been youth oriented. The shift will take place in the coming years as the Baby Boomers, those born between 1946 and 1964, start moving into their sixties. The magic year will be 2006, the year the earliest Boomers hit sixty and start thinking about retirement.

This is a notable date because the Boom generation has always been an intense target of marketers. It is largely because of the cohort's size, more than 78 million people. This group produced the biggest generation of young people going to high school, then to college, then to the workforce. They have always owned the biggest blip on marketers' radar screens.

And in a few years, the Boomers will be the largest generation to move into retirement. It will be interesting to see whether marketers and their agencies will pursue older Boomers as avidly as they pursued them as young Boomers.

Before they sell to aging Boomers, marketers will have to do substantial research on them, especially to dispel myths about older Americans. The new generation of senior citizens will be substantially different from earlier generations. Unquestionably, they will be more concerned with health problems than the eighteen- to thirty-four-year-olds. But they will also be concerned with appearance problems, so they are more likely to purchase hair-coloring products, makeup, skin creams, and the like.

Senior citizens will live longer in retirement than any previous generation. They will be richer and in better physical condition. People over sixty-five are more likely to own their own home than any other age group. They are more likely than eighteen- to thirty-four-year-olds to own securities that have increased greatly in value and to own an individual retirement account. They also are more financially stable and less indebted. They are far less likely to have a car loan, a mortgage, or a credit card balance (*Wall Street Journal*, December 12, 1997).

Here are some other data about the 35 million Americans aged sixty-five and older, derived from the 2000 census:

- For every 100 women over sixty-five, there are only 70 men. The ratio of women to men increases as they get older.
- 14 percent of of Americans sixty-five and older are in the civilian workforce.
- 4.5 percent of them are in nursing homes.
- 49,000 of them were enrolled in colleges in October 2000.
- 72 percent of them voted in the most recent presidential election, a higher turnout than for any other age group.
- 81 percent own their home.

Advertising people say that they have concentrated their efforts on young people because they are more likely to switch brands than older consumers. However, there are strong indications that brand loyalty is declining across all age groups, but most steeply among consumers over sixty (*American Demographics*, November 2000).

This advertiser behavior puzzles Richard A. Lee, principal in High Yield Marketing, a Saint Paul, Minnesota, consulting firm. "It's hard to understand," remarks Lee, "why advertisers still can't bear to tear their sights away from consumers in their teens, twenties, and early thirties, at a time when spending power is becoming progressively more concentrated among those fifty and older" (*American Demographics*, January 1997).

The preponderance of evidence—as well as their own individual aging process—might well persuade marketers to broaden their targets. There is no question the mature market will grow in importance in the years to come as seniors make up an even larger segment of total spending. By 2025, the number of people in the United States aged sixty-five and over will grow by 80 percent, while the number of children and working-age adults will grow by only 15 percent.

This trend should promote the notion of more products aimed at the older market and more advertising appropriate to the age group. Marketers might also consider adapting the old Oldsmobile slogan to this burgeoning sector: "This isn't your father's senior citizen."

THE WOMEN'S MARKET

Women have gone through dramatic role shifts since the end of World War II, but some long-term trends show signs of slowing down or even reversing. The most remarkable aspect of women's evolving social status over the past twenty years was the declining birthrate in the United States, coupled with the increasing percentage of mothers in the workforce. By 1995, 55 percent of women with infants under one year old were back in the workforce. For those with a college education, 68 percent were in the workforce. By 2000, however, the working mother boom started to slow down. Census figures show that the labor force participation of mothers with infant children went down in 1998, the first decline since the bureau started maintaining statistics on working mothers in 1976. "The declines occurred primarily among mothers in the workforce who were thirty years old and over, white women, married women living with their husbands, and women who had completed one or more years of college," Census Bureau analyst Martin O'Connell reports (U.S. Census Bureau press release, October 18, 2001). The same study found no decline in workforce participation by Hispanic and African-American mothers who had a high school diploma or less education. They would tend to be in households with lower incomes, prompting a greater necessity to be in the workforce.

It will take several more years to determine whether the trend toward declining labor force participation will continue, although it is unlikely any percentage decrease would be dramatic. We should also remember that this decline took place during an era of unprecedented growth in the economy, coupled with low unemployment, low inflation, and low interest rates. It will be interesting to see whether the economic slowdown of 2001 to 2002 will prompt more mothers to return to work.

Data on patterns in workforce participation should be important to marketers for a couple of basic reasons. One is that working women and working mothers have very different buying habits from women who do not work outside the home. They spend more money on clothes, prepared foods, transportation, and several other product categories. Working women are also more difficult to reach via traditional media. They certainly don't watch daytime soap operas as much as mothers who are not in the workforce.

As there is a strong correlation between college education and working motherhood, there is also a correlation between higher education and a lower birthrate. The chain of events goes like this: women with a college education tend to get married at a later age and have their first child at a later age. They also have fewer children. What we have now is a steady increase in the number and percentage of women getting college educations. Women account for about 55 percent of the bachelor's degrees awarded in the country, as well as dramatically increased percentages of graduate degrees in law, medicine, business administration, and other areas. As more women attain college educations, this factor will tend to lower the birthrate.

Census Bureau statistics show that for all women, the median age for their first marriage was 25.1 years old in 2000, compared with 20.3 years old in 1950. The median age for college-educated women would be older than the national average.

An important demographic trend affecting women is the steep increase in births to unwed mothers. In 1980, 18.4 percent of U.S. births were to unwed women. By 2000, this had increased to 33.2 percent. Contrary to what many people might believe, the percentage of unwed *teenagers* having babies has declined for several years. The increase is among women in their twenties.

Perhaps related to births by unwed mothers is another trend, the increasing number and percentage of men and women who will never marry. The percentage is expected to top 10 percent. The reasons for this range from increased acceptance of homosexuality to more economic independence for women.

THE YOUTH MARKET

It is almost impossible to perform a quick analysis of young people as consumers because they change habits and opinions so steadily during their formative years. But there is one constant we can assume. At virtually every age, young people are more grown-up than their parents were at the same age. "In the age of the Internet and multimedia, today's youth are growing up quicker," says a press report from Mintel Intelligence Group Ltd. "Their tastes are often more sophisticated, and they have far more choices than their parents at the same age" (Mintel press release, July 2002).

One of the aspects of youth that marketers should consider is the way they consume media. We now have more than a generation of adolescents who were brought up on video games, cell phones, and computers. Sitting down in front of a monitor and keyboard is not a big deal to them.

Perhaps because of this technological orientation, young people tend to shift seamlessly from one medium to the next, even enjoying more than one at the same time. Research in 2001 by Grunwald

Associates reported that among teenage girls using computers at home, 86 percent are listening to the radio at the same time. There is no count on how many are also on the telephone, but parents of teenagers can picture that scene.

I am not aware of any research on this subject, but I have come to identify this characteristic of young people as "sampling." This is not unlike the notion of "grazing" that researchers identified in the 1980s. Americans, especially young professionals, were eating an increasing number of meals away from home. And some of the eating opportunities were not exactly meals: coffee and a bagel for breakfast, a quick burger at McDonald's, a glass of wine and heavy hors d'oeuvres at a reception instead of dinner. Young people today never seem to commit themselves to a single medium, always sampling what is going on at other venues. Perhaps it is a result of always having enjoyed such a huge selection of experiential alternatives. And media seem to be catering to this inclination.

The terrorist attacks of September 11, 2001, prompted television to develop the "crawl," the brief news reports that run at the bottom of the television screen no matter what programming is being aired. This has since developed into a smorgasbord of information one can see regularly on Headline News Network. Here is what is available on a single HNN screen: In the upper right-hand corner of the screen, a newsreader is reporting on an Oklahoma tornado. Immediately to the left of that is a picture of a twister, and under that a quotation, "It sounded like a train going through the house." Immediately below that is the crawl. Below the crawl, sports scores are being flashed up one at a time, including professional and college contests. To the right, under the video of the newsreader, we see various stock market and interest rate indices being flashed. Under that, they are giving the weather, region by region, showing a map of the region and a brief report, like "Cool and rainy." Sometimes they manage to squeeze a burst of celebrity news into this mélange.

This is what I would call the ultimate in information sampling, and it might well be a delivery mechanism for news media that will attract the younger generation. We should also consider *USA Today* and all-news radio formats to be variations of this kind of information sampling. Marketers will also have to determine what kind of advertising messages would complement this style of information delivery.

One good sign for marketers is that the number of young people in the United States will rise at a modest level over the next decade, as opposed to the declines of the 1990s.

THE IMMIGRANT FACTOR

Perhaps the most dramatic shift in U.S. demographics in the past twenty years has been the rapid increase in immigrants, especially from Latin American and Asia. Here is a statistic that might give a more vivid perspective on immigration: Of the elementary and high school students of Asian and Pacific Islander background, 88 percent had at least one foreign-born parent. Of Hispanic students, about 65 percent had a foreign-born parent. Compare that to African-American students, of whom 11 percent had a foreign-born parent, and non-Hispanic white students, with 7 percent.

You can get a look at the ethnic makeup of tomorrow's adult market by assessing today's students. In 1972, 79 percent of elementary and high school students were non-Hispanic white, compared with 63 percent in 1999, and that trend will continue unless there are dramatic changes in the immigration laws (U.S. Census Bureau report, March 13, 2001).

In 1990, demographers were predicting that Hispanics would become the largest minority in the United States by 2010. They were wrong; Hispanics hit that mark by 2002, with a population of 35.3 million (not counting the 3.8 million residents of Puerto Rico), slightly more than the African-American population.

The growth of such a minority market obviously creates challenges for anyone selling goods and services. It takes analysis of language usage, culture, education, and buying habits that are different than the general population. There are several important points to remember about the Hispanic ethnic group:

- 58 percent of all Hispanics in the United States are of Mexican background.
- 50 percent of the nation's Hispanic population lives in California and Texas.
- 90 percent of Hispanics live in metropolitan areas.
- The median age of Hispanics in the United States is 25.8 years, nearly 10 years younger than the nation's overall median.
- Hispanics are overwhelmingly Roman Catholic. The Catholic population in the United States is estimated at 62 million, which means that more than half may be Hispanic.

The Census Bureau has projected the growth among racial groups between 2001 and 2010; see Table 11.3.

Like Hispanics, the Asian population in the United States grew by more than 50 percent in the 1990s, bringing the total number close to 12 million in 2002. According to Census Bureau policy, Asians are included with Pacific Islanders in their ethnic category. The median age of Asians in the United States is 31.1 years, older than for the Hispanics, but still younger than the median of the whole population.

The term *Asian* covers a broad range of people, from Japanese to Middle Easterners, encompassing different cultures, languages, and religions. Asians are unlike any other group of immigrants that have come to the shores of the United States. Rather than "your tired, your poor, your huddled masses yearning to breathe free"—in the words of Emma Lazarus inscribed on the Statue of Liberty—many Asians tend to be highly educated and more affluent than most other ethnic groups. The median family income of Asian households is

TABLE 11.3	PROJECTION OF U.S. POPULATION BY RACE, 2001–2010		
	POPULATION		
Race	July 2001	July 2010	Percent Change
White	227,883,000	241,770,000	6.1%
Black	35,784,000	39,982,000	11.7%
American Indian	2,471,000	2,821,000	14.2%
Asian and Pacific Islander	11,665,000	15,289,000	31.1%
Hispanic	33,616,000	43,688,000	30.0%

Source: U.S. Census Bureau: projections of total resident population by five-year age groups, race, and Hispanic origin with special age categories. Middle Series, 1999 to 2100. (Adapted by the author.)

more than $55,500 a year, and 44 percent of those aged twenty-five and over have college degrees. Here are some other nuggets:

- The largest Asian ethnic group in the United States is Chinese, followed by Indian, Korean, Filipino, and Vietnamese.
- 45 percent of the nation's Asian-born population lives in three metropolitan areas: Los Angeles, New York, and San Francisco.
- 58 percent of the residents of Hawaii report their ethnicity as Asian.
- 10.7 percent of Asians and Pacific Islanders live below the poverty level, exactly half the poverty rate of Hispanics.

Marketing people will face growing numbers and percentages of immigrants in the coming years. How to reach these groups will be a continuing challenge. It will be less difficult for first-generation Hispanics because most of them speak Spanish, while Asians may speak any number of dozens of languages. What comes next is learning how to deal with the second generation and their assimilation into the American culture—if there is such a thing as an American culture.

UNDERSTANDING VALUE SHIFTS

Demographics tells who we are. Psychographics tells how we think and what we believe. The latter may be more difficult to predict than the former, but analyzing and understanding these human characteristics is necessary on several levels of marketing.

In 1997 Northwestern Mutual Life Insurance Company hired the research firm of Louis Harris & Associates to conduct a study of college freshmen who would be the first graduating class of the new millennium. Here are a few indicative results of that survey:

- 77 percent of the students believe strongly that having close family relationships is a key to happiness.
- 61 percent at least somewhat agreed that divorce is an acceptable solution if two people are not happy in a marriage.
- 37 percent strongly agreed that marriage is a cornerstone of social values.
- 68 percent agreed that premarital sex is OK "when two people love each other," and 64 percent agreed that living together before getting married is a good idea.
- 33 percent said that earning a high salary was a very important part of their careers, and only 26 percent agreed that high job prestige was very important (Northwestern Mutual Life Insurance Company, Generation 2001).

These people, by the way, have already graduated, and it will be interesting to see whether their views changed during their college years.

Some of these opinions obviously represent changes from previous generations, such as feelings about premarital sex and living together before getting married. The increase in the percentage of births to unwed women, noted earlier, is evidence of another change in values. Not everybody is comfortable with these shifts, but they cannot be denied. This is part and parcel of the ongoing intergenerational conflicts in the world.

Changes in consumer psychographics are not easy to predict accurately, but marketers have to attempt it to be prepared for the future. They should also understand why these shifts take place.

For example, Census Bureau figures from the early 1990s indicated that 90 percent of young adults expected to get married at some time. The 10 percent share who didn't expect to get married was twice as high as it was in earlier generations. Why? I would guess that greater economic independence for women and increasing acceptance of homosexuality are the two major factors. People are not as pressured by society to get married as they were in earlier eras.

There are many theories about the changing psychographics of Americans. Several are important for marketing and advertising, and the one I would like to mention is the growing importance of experiences, as opposed to money and material goods. I admit it is a pet theory of mine, but I truly believe it can be the basis of marketing.

What is the better way to motivate employees—offer a $500 color television set or a $500 stay at a spa? Unless you have the only remaining American who doesn't have a color TV, the spa would always win out. It is a more powerful incentive because it involves an experience.

When people attain a certain level of wealth and material possessions, the only thing they yearn for are experiences. This includes trekking in Nepal, cruising the Nile, renting a villa in Tuscany, white-water rafting, wall climbing, hot-air ballooning, whale watching, bungee jumping, going to Walt Disney World, or anything else in which a person gets involved with an activity.

Isn't the primary reason people in the upper middle class use illegal drugs the purpose of having a different kind of experience? A millionaire named Steve Fossett spent a good chunk of his money on trying to circumnavigate the globe in a hot-air balloon. He finally did it in 2002. He had earlier swum the English Channel and had run in Alaska's Iditarod dogsled race. The only thing holding back millions of others from these pursuits is that they don't have Fossett's money to burn.

The most talked-about television programs of the last couple of years were so-called reality shows like "Survivor" and "Big Brother." Despite the cheesy nature and low budgets of these programs, the unusual experiences of the participants attracted large audiences, especially the coveted eighteen- to thirty-four-year-olds that marketers lust after.

This isn't necessarily a new idea at all. Many researchers believe that this craving for experiences is akin to a theory promulgated in the mid-1900s by psychologist Abraham Maslow, who determined that humans have a "hierarchy of needs." These range from the basics, like food, safety, belonging, and love, to the highest need, self-actualization. When all of a person's basic needs are taken care of, he or she reaches for something beyond. Today, we might propose that experiences can satisfy that need for self-actualization.

It is ironic that there might be such a sophisticated intellectual theory behind the low-minded television programs, but I bring it up as something for marketing people to chew on as they try to solve the mysteries of an ever-changing consumer universe. Aside from the high-minded stuff, the appeal of these television programs will continue only as long as they can offer push-the-envelope experiences and attract sizable audiences. We can probably predict that the next major step in the world of experiential television will be the offering of simultaneous interactivity to viewers, allowing them to participate in the programs.

ANOTHER VOICE . . .

Advertising Loves to Entertain; Its Real Objective Should Be to Generate Excitement

STEPHEN F. UNWIN

We've neglected consumer desire. That's why consumers are taking an extended holiday in this recession. Why the Web was wiped out overnight. Why many Christmas retailers and resorts have gone into mourning.

Today's advertising is so busy looking over its shoulder to see what analysts are saying about its company's stock value, and what its competitors are saying in their ads, that the consumer has been left out of the loop. It offers savings and discounts but little pizzazz to make us want to get the product into our hands as soon as we possibly can. Passion of ownership and ecstasy of use take a back seat.

Today's consumers are disenchanted with goods and services per se and long only for that usurper of mass consumption—money. Let's face it. We've become a nation of money collectors now. We've given up the sheer joy of gathering goods. The excitement is all in the extended credit, the colossal savings, and no payments until 2003— not in the products themselves.

Back in the seventies, I wrote an article for *Journal of Marketing* called "The Synchronistic Theory of Advertising." It said the function of advertising was to speed up mass consumption to keep it in balance with mass production. Mass equals speed, and we'd better make sure consumers are primed to acquire the fruits of the advanced economy. The balancing act between manufacturer supply and consumer demand is not advertising's job anymore. That's done by just-in-time production, delivery, and zero financing. Today's advertising often seems to punish consumers, not praise them or encourage them to trade up to better and better things.

Where are the sexologists who steered our sublimated drives toward metal and plastic beauties? Where is Dichter, the dean of motivation? Ogilvy, the king of image? Reeves, the scientist of unique selling propositions? And Ries, the perpetrator of positioning? Do we pay court to any of them? Do we even know them or what they stood for?

This perhaps explains why so many ads today have joined the entertainment industry. TV has sports entertainment, courtroom entertainment, news entertainment. Now it has its share of corporate entertainment. They often treat their business as such a huge joke; the brand, the brand benefit, and even its name are drowned in laughter. Some ads tell riddles. They keep us all guessing what it's for and even who made it until way past the end. Other ads congratulate and self-congratulate. They hand out awards. They preen and pose and patronize.

Ads have become their own currency. They are not cost-efficient, proactive marketing tools anymore. Some advertisers have handed their production over to Hollywood. Hollywood revels in the opportunity to direct commercial epics with casts of thousands, special effects, and mini dramas, but "Where's the beef?"

Advertising production costs must be the most inflationary in the entire economy. As the pioneer retailer John

Wanamaker is credited with saying, "We know half of our advertising is wasted . . ." But this is ridiculous!

HOUSE OF CARDS

Why then, do we ask, did the Web industry collapse like a house of cards? Did no one know what the sites were for and what really was the unique benefit? Were we expected to become a nation of stay-at-homes and give up our personal transportation, our highways, and our malls?

Super affluence has bred a very cost-conscious, non-brand-conscious consumer. After a dozen mergers, it's difficult to maintain a semblance of brand identity. When commoditization sets in and everything is a necessity, there's not much excitement left. The only concern is, "How much?" We're back to Adam Smith and his bushels of wheat. Price and price promotion have taken over from benefit promotion in the marketing mix.

But advertising works best when it is building consumer awareness, trial, and repeat use in brand-new industries for new products and services that people have only imagined before. With the surge in technological productivity, fewer and fewer people need to be employed in agriculture, manufacturing, and now in services. What work will we all do? Expand what we have already begun, providing new experiences, new cultural opportunities, new spiritual programs, new environmental revolutions, and many other new fields. The number of personal coaches just went up 1,000 percent in five years. There's a museum-building boom going on in the South. Today's Web surfers want religious information more than auctions or banks. Even box-car city has embarked on a fast-track manufacturing program to reintroduce America to sleek, sexy, "got to have one" new models.

This is advertising's new frontier, getting people to want to buy what they have never had before.

The synchronistic theory was right. Advertising does do a balancing act between mass production and mass consumption, supply and demand. It just changed its direction 180 degrees. Now we must get out of reverse to fast forward and create real, new wealth for demanding consumers.

Stephen F. Unwin (wss1110@hotmail.com), a former international advertising executive and advertising educator, is president of Business Dynamics, an advertising and marketing consultancy in Kingwood, Texas. This piece originally appeared as a "Viewpoint" article in the February 25, 2002, issue of Advertising Age.

DOES ADVERTISING HAVE A FUTURE?

The Road Ahead Is Curvy and Treacherous, and Good Road Maps Are in Short Supply

Yes, the title of this chapter is tongue-in-cheek. Advertising does have a future. However, when I was doing initial research and interviews for this book and would tell people in the advertising world what its title was to be, more than once the question snapped back to me was, "You mean we are actually going to have a future in this business?"

I realize they were joking. But the frequency of responses like that confirmed my earliest notion that many practitioners of the various marketing arts are more than a bit insecure about where advertising is headed. This is not unexpected. The changes in the last twenty years, even ten years, have been dramatic and unsettling.

Most people don't like change. Especially not if they're people who enjoy what they are doing, are pretty good at it, and are making a good living from it. It is tough to imagine that some or all of that will go away. I have lived through that kind of change. Perhaps the most difficult period in my life was in early 1978. I was writing a daily advertising and marketing column for the *Chicago Daily News*. It was a terrific newspaper with an outstanding tradition of great journalism and more than a dozen Pulitzer prizes to prove it. We had a gifted staff of journalists who actually respected and liked each other. (All these years later, we still have a monthly "alumni" newsletter and get together at least once a year.)

More than that, I was performing a job that I loved. The advertising business at that time was filled with interesting and exciting people. They gave great parties and created breakthrough advertising. Life was good. And then, one day, the publisher of the newspaper came into the city room and announced that he was going to close the place down.

Nobody wants to go through that kind of change. I didn't like it, and it took many months and a couple of job changes before I felt comfortable and secure again.

This is not to say that agencies are going to start closing left and right the way afternoon newspapers did in the 1960s and 1970s. But it is totally certain that the agency business, after a decade of change, is going to see even more change in the future. I firmly believe that the notion of the advertising agency will have to go through a dramatic redefinition and reinvention in order to survive and prosper in the coming years.

This is not a revelation to those in the business. They have already gone through a great deal of trauma because of the rapid consolidation of the agency business. I know several top agency people who are conscientiously working on new approaches to their business and their companies. I applaud them.

This notion of redefinition, in fact, was perhaps the key element in the working title for this book. I originally considered such titles as *The Redefinition of Advertising* or *Advertising Redefined*. One of my suggestions was *Advertising: New and Improved! Or Is It?* Another was *They Don't Call It the Ad Game Anymore*. These ideas were all relegated to the editing floor—maybe with good reason.

Nevertheless, it is imperative that any business facing a torrent of new challenges needs to redefine what function it serves for its clients. An industry might thrive for decades because of the service it performs. But if it is being threatened because of new competition, an evaporating market, a change in consumer attitudes, remarkable new technology, tremendous consolidation, or any other such monumental shift, the only alternatives available hearken back to that headline on my 1992 article in *Advertising Age*: "Change or Die."

So what does the future hold for all of the elements in this industry? We're not soothsayers, but we should be able to read the trends and make educated guesses about where we are going. Let's take a look at various elements of the business individually and try to compose reasonable scenarios for the next five years.

ADVERTISING AGENCIES

Because of the extensive consolidation that has taken place in the last decade, further consolidation will take place at a slower rate in the immediate future. Part of this is a reaction to the government's closer scrutiny of the mergers because of the Enron debacle. A pause in consolidation at this point is also good because it will give the acquirers an opportunity to digest the new properties and position them efficiently within the corporate umbrella.

Even at a slower pace, there will be more mergers and acquisitions, but it is doubtful there will be another major holding company formed that compares with the current Big Four.

The bigger question regarding structure is whether the four holding companies will remain intact. I don't think they will. These are all global conglomerates made up of dozens of different companies of different sizes, different cultures, and different personalities. Not all marriages are made in heaven, no matter how happy the couple looked on their wedding day.

Many of these acquisitions took place because the former owners were ready to retire and were offered an opportunity to get an equitable compensation for their ownership. The operations acquired under these circumstances are more likely to remain within the holding companies, running under new management.

The situation is different for operations with a strong entrepreneurial leader who agreed to the acquisition because it would give the company access to more capital or to bigger clients. It is not unusual for a management like this to feel bridled by a corporate hierarchy. The former owners might choose to buy themselves back from the parent. This is especially true if a declining stock market has lowered the value of the subsidiary. We can almost guarantee there will be circumstances like these in the next couple of years. Above all, sometimes an acquired unit simply doesn't fit into the corporate puzzle the way it appeared before the merger.

It also isn't impossible that we might see a major agency unit break away from its parent holding company in the near future. This could be an advertising agency with a strong CEO who doesn't fit into the corporate structure. It is less likely to happen with a company that was publicly held before the acquisition, but defections have occurred in other industries, and they could also happen in advertising.

It is also likely that a nonadvertising subsidiary might break away because it did not benefit from corporate ownership. This is all part of life in the publicly held lane.

More likely, though, is that it will become more common for clients to dictate the structure and ownership of their advertising agencies. Rather than have an account simply move from one agency to another, we can anticipate a situation in which a major client dissatisfied with its holding company relationship might engineer the defection of its agency staff and underwrite the formation of a new agency. This has already happened in the past because of perceived client conflict, and it will happen in the future as long as the holding companies are handling hundreds of brands and companies.

These freestanding, client-sponsored agencies will have no need to be part of any of the holding companies. The holding companies really will have no advantages to offer these breakaway shops. The logical question to ask is whether clients enjoy any benefits by doing business with an advertising agency or any other marketing services unit of a holding company. I don't think so.

WHO WILL HANDLE INTEGRATION?

What is yet to be determined is how well the holding companies will grapple with the challenge of integration of their services. Over the years, they have bought up a wide variety of companies in different aspects of the marketing business, but there has not been a great deal of coordination among the various disciplines.

As a couple of forward-thinking agency executives were quoted as saying early in this book, there is a need for some kind of general contractor or orchestra conductor to direct strategies for their clients and to coordinate the various marketing elements to form a cohesive campaign.

In many other business disciplines, this is the kind of activity that outside management consultants might normally perform. The holding companies would like to fill this vacuum, but they face an uphill struggle for a couple of reasons. The first is that they tend to be dominated by their advertising agency components, rather than their direct-marketing, sales promotion, or Web developer components. Another problem is the perception that a holding company could not be very objective in assembling the most effective network of companies to work on a client's campaign. Clients would assume their agency would have a vested interest in assigning work only to other companies within the holding company. So far, the clients would be pretty accurate in that assessment.

The ultimate threat to this position by the holding companies is that some well-known, highly respected management consulting firms would build a substantial practice in marketing management. The consultants could position themselves to be the objective overseers of corporate marketing strategy, usurping a crucial role that the holding companies would dearly love to fill.

This is not unlike the function that management consultants and public accounting firms developed years ago in strategic management of technology and information services. They were not players in the technology business, so they were able to address the needs of a client with no preconceived notions or prejudices. And the clients loved this impartiality.

At the same time, it is possible that the consultants specializing in agency search might also try to usurp this function of strategic integration. That scenario, however, is less likely. Although they have developed their specific practices in agency evaluation and selection, they generally lack the long-established relationship with corporate clients as general consultants.

The major management consultants are in a more advantageous position to assume this role because they are already relating to corporate managers at the highest levels. They are already entrusted with some of the most sensitive research and analysis, probing the deepest secrets and pointing out the most serious weaknesses of a corporation. They are also more likely to be considered impartial by their clients because they aren't in the marketing business themselves.

It is also possible that corporate clients might try to establish this kind of strategic planning function internally. This is especially true at large corporations with many different subsidiaries, brands, and products. The internal strategy group could operate as a kind of "SWAT team," called in by various divisions to help develop campaigns, positioning, creative strategy, or whatever the unit needs.

There is, of course, always a political situation within corporations that works against this kind of internal function. There is also the downside of what may happen if the SWAT team totally misses its mark and comes up with an integrated campaign that turns out to be a bummer. It's more difficult to fire employees than outside contractors.

This function of coordination and integration will first be demonstrated in the client-sponsored breakaway agencies previously mentioned. They would be best suited for the role because they are outside the client's corporate realm yet in the best position to oversee all of the various marketing functions. They probably won't even be called ad agencies anymore.

As you can see, the future of this strategic function is still a bit murky. If it is ultimately developed by the holding companies, it seems that it would have to exist as an entity separate from any other unit of the holding company. It has to be more than a bunch of former ad agency guys putting out a new shingle. What may eventually happen is that one or more of the holding companies might acquire general consulting firms and set up independent operations. You will know they are independent when they start recommending that part of a client's work be assigned to units of a different holding company.

MEDIA BUYING MOVES TO THE FOREFRONT

When I started covering the advertising business nearly thirty-five years ago, the media-buying function was firmly ensconced in the agencies. Although the media department was responsible for generating virtually all of the agency's revenues, its responsibilities were relegated to newcomers in the business, young people right out of college, or women who had moved up from clerical levels.

The situation was so bad that the *New York Times* ran a major article years ago about twenty-two-year-olds who were responsible for buying millions of dollars' worth of media. Television was the biggest recipient of their spending, and the selection was based on how many rating points the programs would produce. That was all pretty easy.

At least these media buyers were generally television viewers and had some notion of the programming. Magazines were a different matter. If you were one of the weekly newsmagazines or *Rolling Stone*, you were OK. They knew who you were. But if you were selling space in a business publication, especially a business-to-business publication, there was little or no chance that the young media buyers even glanced at the free subscription you sent them.

I admit that this might be somewhat of an overstatement. I did run into several media directors—but far fewer media buyers or planners—who were actually interested in what we were doing in the early days of *Crain's Chicago Business*. We were not only trying to sell our publication, but the whole notion of regional business publishing. I can't tell you how often the first question our salespeople would get from a media buyer was, "So, what makes you different from the *Wall Street Journal*?"

All of this has changed, of course, as media buying has undergone the most dramatic transition of any element in the marketing arena. Media buying has largely been pulled away from ad agencies, and media commission levels have been cut by 75 percent or more. More than that, though, media buying has become incredibly more complicated than it was thirty-five years ago, when the three television networks ruled the advertising world. This growing complexity of the media world will make the media-buying function even more important in the years to come as the range of new media continues to expand.

It is certain that media buying will become more strategic as this function becomes more involved in the selection of sales promotion, direct marketing, interactive, and other nonadvertising areas. And clients will increase their demand for integrated marketing communications, a programmed approach that would be directed by media buyers.

THE BATTLE FOR CONSUMER ATTENTION

It is fair to say that the arena for the communications challenge of the future will be a battle for consumer attention. No single medium will dominate, as television did between the 1960s and 1990s. There will always be mass markets, but advertisers will not be able to reach them through mass communications, except for those few events that can draw a huge audience.

This reality will require more emphasis on what were formerly below-the-line activities, such as direct marketing and sales promotion. Except for possible government tightening of privacy laws in the United States, direct marketing will continue to expand, but most of the expansion will be beyond the most traditional forms of mass mailings, telemarketing, and E-mail solicitations. The situation will be different in Europe, where more stringent privacy laws already exist and are not likely to be relaxed.

Here is what appears likely for other forms of marketing:

- *Place-based marketing* will become increasingly important as a form of direct response. Being able to make contact with potential consumers in airports, airplanes, taxicabs, and hotels is one way to avoid the privacy laws while still zeroing in on the traveling market. Interactive kiosks will be installed in a variety of venues and will be as common as ATMs.

- *Event marketing* will continue to grow as advertisers look for opportunities to communicate with consumers on a one-to-one basis. Events in which consumers self-select whether they attend will multiply. These are already visible in free investment seminars by stock brokerages, golfing clinics by equipment marketers, and those ubiquitous free minivacations offered by real estate developers.

- *Sponsorship* of public venues also will increase and will expand from sports arenas to virtually any place that people congregate. An example is the Roundabout Theatre Company in New York, which performs at the American Airlines Theatre on Broadway. Chicago has not only the Cadillac Palace Theater, but also the Ford Center for the Performing Arts at the Oriental Theater, illustrating that the car companies are already into the game.

- *Cobranding and comarketing* of different but complementary products and services will increase. A cigar company will hook up with a cognac company and stage an event at a hotel or a restaurant, creating a trio of marketers all out to snare the same demographic audience. The quest in all of these ventures will be to isolate a core of top prospects and put them in a situation where they are exposed to the client's brands and products, away from the competitive nature of advertising in the traditional media.

- *Public relations* will become more common, if for no other reason than there are more media at PR practitioners' disposal, and it will be easier to obtain exposure for clients than it is to get time on the networks and space in the national magazines. Just imagine what the proliferation of regional business publications has done to expand the opportunities for public relations efforts. There are probably more than two hundred of these journals in the United States, compared with only a handful of national business publications.

TELEVISION IN THE POST-TELEVISION ERA

It would be an obvious overstatement to say that television is going to fade away. But it is not an overstatement to predict that the medium will go through the same kind of reinvention that radio was forced to undergo when it was undercut by television in the 1950s.

Network broadcasting in most cases will continue to offer least-common-denominator programming. The networks' mission is to aggregate as many eyeballs as they can, regardless of the quality of the audience. Television is all about ratings.

Cable and satellite networks also like big audience numbers, but they have an advantage in being a dual-revenue system, getting subscription and pay-per-view money as well as advertising revenues. The next big movement, though, will be adding interactivity to cable and satellite.

This will add all kinds of nuances to the notion of television, including having viewers take part in the programming, especially in shows without a predetermined ending. This type of program could be reminiscent of one of the most popular stage plays of the last twenty years, "The Mystery of Edwin Drood." The play is based on Charles Dickens's last novel, but Dickens died before he could finish the book. The producers used the manuscript to set the first part of the play, a mystery in which Drood is murdered. Toward the end of the play, the audience is polled to see whom they think was the murderer. The cast then finishes the play with a denouement featuring the murderer chosen by the audience. Interactivity, even in entertainment, can be an effective attraction.

This could also work with quiz shows, which seem to have a never-ending status on television, not only in the United States but in virtually every country of the world. It might be possible for some viewers to play "Who Wants to Be a Millionaire?" along with a studio contestant. Interactive television, at least in its early days, will attract large audiences, if only for the novelty aspect. But when viewers tire of a program, programming creativity will be necessary to hook them again.

Gambling activity is very popular on the Internet, although it is attacked by moralists and is illegal in many places. It would be technologically possible to have interactive gambling on television, but chances are the authorities would never give their approval.

WILL WE HAVE A POST-PRINT AGE?

I have spent more than half of my life as a print journalist, so I have a vested interest in the future of print. I don't want to see print fade away as a medium, and it certainly will not do so within our five-year outlook.

Beyond that, print has problems, and these problems do not involve the quality of the writing or the information, but mostly the distribution system. At greatest risk are newspapers. Their inherent weakness is that they are captives of nineteenth- and twentieth-century practices. They cut down trees, put ink on them, and use trucks to dispense these unwieldy publications throughout a metropolitan area.

A pithy colleague of mine from the *Chicago Daily News* was once asked what was the greatest technological advance in journalism in the twentieth century. Without a beat, he quipped, "Air conditioning. It's much more comfortable in newsrooms than it was in the old days."

It's not that bad, but it's close. Daily journalism has been made more efficient by all kinds of technological advances, from the computer to the cell phone to the Internet. But the essence of a newspaper is still reduced to the final act of printing and putting those finished copies on trucks that barrel through a city's streets with their cargo of information.

Newspapers have two choices. If they want to continue to be *news*papers, they will have to find a distribution system that gets the news to their subscribers before they get it from other sources. This pretty much rules out printing. It is very possible that some of the experiments with PDF delivery of newspapers will prove to be successful. But even here, newspapers will have to tailor their product for this new medium.

If they want to continue being distributed via the current archaic system, then they will have to change the nature of the product they deliver to their readers. In most cases, the product isn't news, but it can be business information, entertainment, advice, literature, or anything else the reader needs.

Magazines are in a different position because they are not as reliant on timely delivery as newspapers. But this doesn't mean they are guaranteed an existence throughout the twenty-first century. My rule of thumb in the magazine world is that the bigger the circulation, the greater the challenge to survive.

The mass national magazines have suffered the most since the introduction of television. Niche publications have fared far better.

But the Internet will have an impact on niche publications similar to that of television on mass magazines. Once again, it is time for magazines to redefine themselves.

Special-interest and special-audience magazines have the brightest future. But they cannot rely on print alone. They will have to create communities, rather than mailing lists. They will have to employ multimedia measures, including Internet and perhaps broadcast modes to serve their audiences. Many are doing this already, but more will have to do this for survival.

■ ■ ■ ■

As I stated early in this book, one medium has never destroyed another medium. Individual publications may have folded because of new competition, but the print medium itself has not gone away, and some magazines are thriving.

The future of any business, industry, or profession would be more secure if its participants adhered to the basic techniques of good management. And what do we manage? We manage people. We manage money. We manage technology. We manage real estate. But what we must really learn to manage is *change*.

Change is all around us. It never stops. We have different markets, different competitors, different customers, different values, different technologies. The way we will survive over the next five years and beyond is by managing this never-ending current of change. We must learn how to anticipate the change, how to recognize it, and how to respond to it. That may allow us to survive.

But there can be one more, higher level of accomplishment: we can *create* the change in the marketplace. We can have competitors respond to us, instead of vice versa. We can build new technology, explore new markets, think and act in new and different ways. That kind of attitude and action would allow us not only to survive, but to thrive for decades to come.

REFERENCE LIST

Advertising Age, April 22, 2002. "Top media specialist agencies," p. S-14.

————, May 20, 2002. "Top marketing services agencies," p. S-4.

————, June 1, 1964. "Lois hits critics of shops that go public," p. 8.

Agri-Food Trade Service website (agri-trade.com), November 2000. "The U.S. market for private-label foods."

Automotive News Databook, 2002.

Beer Institute website (beerinstitute.org), 2002.

Electronic Media, June 10, 2002. "Briefly noted," p. 3.

EMarketer, October 1, 2002. "U.S. consumer online buying and shopping grid."

Entry Media Incorporated website (entrymedia.com).

Francese, Peter, March 23, 1998. "The gray continent," *Wall Street Journal*, p. A-22.

Friedman, Wayne, September 23, 2002. "Madison and Vine: Product placements rise at CBS." *Advertising Age*, p. 8.

Gardyn, Rebecca, October 2000. "Moving targets," *American Demographics*, p.32.

Goldsborough, Robert, March 18, 2002. "Marion Harper Jr.: from visionary leader to fallen idol to resurrected innovator." *Advertising Age*, p. C-22.

Inside Media, April 26, 1995. "It can happen here," p. 29.

International Data Corp., April 3, 2002. "U.S. online airline ticket sales, by sales channel, 2000–2005," eMarketer website (emarketer.com).

Jupiter Research 2001, derived by eMarketer.

Kramer, Staci, April 29, 2002. "VOD's ad-skipping irks Kellner," Cable World website (kagan.com).

Lee, Richard A., January 1997. "The youth bias in advertising," *American Demographics*, p. 47.

Leidig, Mike, August 31, 2002. "Advertising-supported system of free bikes is back on track in Vienna." *Advertising Age*'s Daily World Wire.

Mayer, Martin, November 21, 1973. "How admen see their business—getting better," *Advertising Age*, p. 50.

MBIQ Media Consumption Study, November 2001. Online Publishers' Association.

Mintel International Group Ltd., July 25, 2002. News release, "Are kids growing up too soon?"

Myers, Jack, March 18, 2002. "Mid-sized media buying groups lead in creative applications," *Jack Myers Report*.

Neff, Jack, June 4, 2001. "Feeling the squeeze," *Advertising Age*, p. 1.

Newbart, Dave, September 23, 2002. "NUTV lets students watch cable on PC," *Chicago Sun-Times*, p. 9.

Northwestern Mutual Life Insurance Co., 1997. "Generation 2000" survey conducted by Louis Harris & Associates.

O'Dwyer, Gerard, August 8, 2002. "Danish company sells advertising space on prams," *Advertising Age*'s Daily World Wire.

Ostrow, Joanne, July 16, 2002. "'TV executives divided on ad-zapping devices," *Denver Post Online* (denverpost.com).

Pew Research Center for the People and the Press, June 9, 2002. Survey, "Public's news habits little changed by September 11."

Tedeschi, Bob, March 25, 2002. "The catalog business J. Crew reaches a milestone as its sales over the Web exceed sales from its catalog." The *New York Times*, p. C6.

Thompson, Stephanie, April 29, 2002. "Wal-Mart tops list for new food lines," *Advertising Age*, p. 4.

U.S. Census Bureau, October 18, 2001. Press release, "Labor force participation for mothers with infants declines for first time."

U.S. Census Bureau, March 2001. Census 2000 brief, "Overview of race and Hispanic origin."

Vranica, Suzanne, July 31, 2002. "The guy showing off his hot new phone may be a shill," *Wall Street Journal*, p. B-1.

Wall Street Journal, December 12, 1997. "Balance sheet, savings and debt by generation," p. R-5.

World Federation of Advertisers, September 24, 2001. Press release, "Revolution in agency pay in Europe."

INDEX